Then There Was Her

Then There Was Her

SOPHIE CACHIA

**SIMON &
SCHUSTER**

London · New York · Sydney · Toronto · New Delhi

THEN THERE WAS HER
First published in Australia in 2022 by
Simon & Schuster (Australia) Pty Limited
Suite 19A, Level 1, Building C, 450 Miller Street,
Cammeray, NSW 2062

10 9 8 7 6 5 4 3 2

Sydney New York London Toronto New Delhi
Visit our website at www.simonandschuster.com.au

 A catalogue record for this
book is available from the
National Library of Australia

ISBN: 9781761103193

Project Editor: Alix Nicholson
Cover design: Meng Koach
Cover photography: Regina Karon, Karon Photography
Typeset by Midland Typesetters, Australia
Printed and bound in Australia by Griffin Press

 The paper this book is printed on is certified against the
Forest Stewardship Council® Standards. Griffin Press holds
chain of custody certification SGSHK-COC-005088. FSC®
promotes environmentally responsible, socially beneficial
and economically viable management of the world's forests

Bobby Mac, Florence Margaret and my future babies . . .
For changing my entire perspective on life and giving me
the greatest honour in life.
My only wish for you is that you live happy,
whatever that looks like.
Mumma will never judge you. Instead, I promise to be
forever inspired by you.
Every day is for you.

Jaryd
My first true love. Thank you for teaching me about what
real family and true loyalty means.
I will love you forever.

Mum and Dad
For the most incredible childhood memories.
I'm sorry it took me becoming a parent myself to appreciate
the pressures and sacrifices you made for me and my
three sisters. I now live to create as many of these
as I can for my own babies.

BK
For ringing me at the exact moment I needed you to.
I can't imagine my life without you, nor do I ever want to.

Foreword

Bruce Kaider

It was a Monday afternoon in mid-2019 and I had taken my trusty lieutenant of nearly sixteen years out for lunch to celebrate her birthday. While eating, we spoke about how I wanted to diversify our business and bring on more clients who worked outside the sports environment we'd traditionally focused on. I was looking to shift focus to include entertainment and the new digital world that was taking over everything we do.

'Sophie Cachia has recently left her agent – she posted it on her Instagram page,' was the reply my co-worker gave to my long-winded spiel.

Now, the name was familiar, but I did need a bit of prompting as to who this 'Sophie Cachia' person actually was, so I pulled up her Instagram page and we started scrolling. I would be lying if I said I didn't notice her looks before anything else – a typical male response, some would say.

'Sophie is hot,' I said openly to my colleague of that first impression, but for the next thirty minutes, as we perused her page searching for signs that she could be a good fit for our business, I realised there seemed to be so much more to this person than a pretty face.

'Send her an email,' my colleague suggested. 'What have you got to lose?'

Absolutely nothing!

Hey Sophie,

Hope you are well?

I read with interest that you don't currently have a manager. I would love to sit down with you and see what it was that didn't work with your last manager, and if you are open to working with a management group.

I have been an agent for 15+ years and my company represents talent in a range of disciplines.

Our office in Melbourne is in Essendon. Let me know if you have any interest in having a chat over a coffee sometime. There's a great place right near our office that is perfect for a casual catch up. Looking forward to hearing from you.

Regards,
Bruce Kaider

After lunch, we headed back to the office and I was curious to see if the mysterious 'Sophie' would email us back or if my note would get lost in the digital ether, which so often happens. I have a rule that I often reflect on, especially in our line of work: when approaching a prospective client, I believe their response says a lot about the genuine chance of them becoming a part of our business. If they respond, 'Thanks but no thanks,' they are either happy, can't be fucked taking another meeting, or they're content with the devil they know. If they respond that they would be happy to catch up for a coffee, then it's in our hands – they have likely looked over our website and social media platforms, have developed an interest in understanding how we can help them, and the game is ours to win or lose.

At 4.08pm, I received a reply.

Hi Bruce,
Thanks for getting in touch.
Would be happy to have a coffee, and I'm an Essendon local –
how good!
What's next week like for you?
Thanks,
Soph

I couldn't have known as we sat down for coffee a few days later that I was meeting a woman who is now not only an amazingly talent client, but also someone I call one of my very best friends.

When Sophie talks about her family, her business, her relationships, or digital marketing, the energy and passion that bursts out of her is overwhelmingly infectious – but she's not all talk. Sophie is as studious as she is driven; always well-researched and prepared for a balanced discussion (or a convincing argument – anyone who truly knows her will have experienced this firsthand and will no doubt be grinning at reading this!).

For me, the words 'authentic', 'honest', 'raw' and 'insightful' come to mind when I think of Sophie Cachia. I could cite countless examples of times she's displayed all these qualities, and you only need to visit her various social media platforms to experience any one of them. Her ability to build an audience of like-minded fans, followers and friends who are as inspired as she is – that's an amazing skill, as is her knack for inspiring others (myself included) to be better, to do better and to always challenge the status quo. It's a quality that should feature in a new-world version of the classic *How to Win Friends and Influence People*.

Then There was Her, as the title suggests, takes the reader on a journey of exploration, maturation, human dynamics, love and loss, as seen through the eyes of a young girl, an adolescent, a young mum and wife, a loving partner, and, perhaps above all, a woman who is determined to be unbound by social norms. Sophie's ability to share her experiences and articulate them in a way that makes you feel you are there, living them alongside her, aligns with her expressive, unique and creative way of storytelling – something those close to her are privileged to experience on a day-to-day basis. If you have enjoyed following Soph on social media, or listening to her various podcasts, you will know her distinctive voice, and you will love delving deeper into what has inspired this incredible lady, and the experiences that have helped shape and transform her into the person she is today.

It is now 2022, and Sophie and I have been working together for more than two years. I could never have imagined that the woman who met me for a coffee back in 2019 would become such a loyal friend and supporter. She is someone who will support the people she loves unconditionally, refraining from any judgement, but she is also willing to give feedback and keep you in check if it's required. When you find people like this – like Soph – and you also enjoy happen to enjoy their company, you find yourself wanting to spend more time in their presence, and there are few people whose presence I enjoy more than hers.

Sophie, thank you for asking me to write your foreword. Ours has been and continues to be an eventful but hugely rewarding journey. From the moment we first spoke about this project, I knew that the end result would be a book that speaks to so many different audiences, and one that will inspire and empower those who read it to be true to themselves, dare to dream and live with no regrets.

I can't wait to see what 'her' next move will be.

Bruce Kaider x

Jaryd

From the moment my wife told me she was attracted to a woman I knew our relationship was going to change dramatically.

But did I think that would kick off a series of events that would eventually lead to our marriage breaking down? Not for a second.

She walked in one evening after speaking on a panel and I could just tell something was different. I'd never seen her like this before.

'I had the strangest thing happen to me tonight,' she said, sounding confused and excited. 'I met this woman. And I was . . . attracted to her. I don't know what it was. I've never felt like this before, but I was really turned on by this woman.'

I wasn't surprised at all that she told me, because honesty was always a huge part of our relationship.

'It was kind of like meeting a female version of you, actually. It was weird.'

I couldn't have guessed how important that night would be in either of our lives, but I did know that things were about to become very different. I could see it in her eyes: she was taken by this person. There was something in the way she spoke, in her body language that told me this was a big deal. And I know Sophie – she's an extremely driven person, and if she wants to do something, she'll do it and she'll do it well. I've never met anyone like her and I commend and respect her for it. But I knew that she was going to need to follow this thing and see where it would lead her. It was just in her nature.

I wasn't worried; not exactly. But I knew in the back of my mind, that something was going to happen; that there was no way this would be our last conversation about it. Of course, I had no idea where it would go, but knowing how spiritual Sophie is, I was certain it wouldn't be a one-night flirtation. When something that momentous happens to her, she needs to explore, and I was sure that she would be driven to suss out what that experience had meant and why she'd felt that way about another woman.

Over the months that followed, I could tell it was playing on her mind as the two of them struck up a bit of a friendship. Soph would speak about how attractive this girl was – and she was right, this woman was hot – pointing out features she loved, dropping little comments here and there, and we'd go together to watch her play footy. They were hanging out a bit, which I was totally on board with – like I said, we were always very honest – and I was never jealous. That's just not me.

I remember when she came in one morning after a big night out – it was the morning of our son's birthday party and she'd gone out with some friends the night before. She'd crawled into bed at, like, 5am so hungover, and then came in to talk to me while I was in the shower a couple of hours later. She was hunched over, clearly feeling like shit, but she had this little smirk on her face.

'I've got to tell you something,' she started.

'You kissed her, didn't you?!'

She burst out laughing.

'I'm not an idiot,' I laughed. 'I knew something was going to happen, the way you kept talking about her! So . . . what was it like?' Again, that's just how we were – we told each other everything. She was hungover as all hell telling me about it, sharing exactly what had happened, and it was so clear in that moment that things were going to change – and they were going to change quickly. Back then, she was so straight, so for her to then be kissing a woman was big. I just knew it wasn't nothing.

Anyway, Soph was like the walking dead, and we had to get out of the house and get our kids to our son Bobby's birthday party, so we didn't talk about it any more until we were back home, having a cigarette out the back. It became pretty clear that she was more confused by this situation than anything. There was no malicious intent from her, and as this thing went on and continued to develop, Soph was more puzzled than I was – so through the whole process, I just tried to put myself in her shoes and think about how she was coping. She was so open and honest about everything with me, and there was no point in me getting upset – it wouldn't have achieved anything. I wasn't jealous at all, probably because I also wasn't surprised. Even though I was her husband and we were living under one roof, I didn't see it as my place to pry and ask questions the whole time. If Soph wanted to come to me and talk to me about it, then she did, and I'd just sit and listen. I left it up to her to open up to me when she felt comfortable because if I had been constantly asking questions, she would have thought I was cracking the shits or getting upset and I think that would've probably pushed her away. As far as I was concerned, the ball was in her court with how she wanted to express herself and talk about the situation she was in.

On the outside it probably looked like we had it all. And we did have it good, we were the envy of all our couple friends – great sex life, two beautiful kids, a home together . . . But I was dealing with some of my own issues that were completely separate to what Soph was going through with her sexuality and her exploring herself. And those two things – Soph's self-discovery and my own problems – they came to a head in 2019, months after she'd discovered her attraction to women.

Around the end of 2018, Sophie came to me and said things needed to change with us. To be honest, I didn't see it coming, I really didn't, despite her starting to have more experiences with women. Looking back, I might've gotten a little comfortable in the relationship, a little complacent, but it was sort of where we were in that moment. I was the stay-at-home dad and at the time I was also going through the process to join the police force. I got to the last stage of applying and was knocked back for reasons that were outside my control – to do with family history, relatives that had been in trouble with the law. I was open and honest in declaring that and I was pretty shattered when I was refused because of things other people had done.

I think that's where my problems really started. I was always the kid that wanted to be a police officer. Still inside me now, as a 30-year-old man, that eight-year-old boy is running around the house with his plastic gun on his hip, his badge, his handcuffs, wanting to be a copper. I knew I'd make a fucking excellent police officer, too, and it's a career that can open so many doors. I was desperate to get in. And then when I didn't, I was completely lost. I'd come from playing AFL football, professional football, and as an athlete,

I'd developed a particular mindset, which I still have. When you leave that high-intensity world and you come back to the everyday nine-to-five, it's really hard to figure out where you fit. Where am I going to get my kick from? How am I going to fuel that fire inside me? Trying to find passion that resembles training and playing at such high intensity is really tough, and when the only thing I ever wanted to do was taken away, I felt like I'd lost my purpose in life.

I never let Sophie in on how bad I was. She knew I was struggling, but while all of this was going on for me, she was also going through her own stuff. She was out there, exploring, on this amazing journey of self-discovery, at the same time forging out her career and in such a motivated headspace. Meanwhile, I was going in the complete opposite direction.

Soph was earning great money, but it got to the point to where she didn't want all the financial pressure on her, so I went and got a job as an orderly at a hospital. The pay wasn't amazing but having the second income was handy. The hours were good, it was shift work, so it was pretty flexible. But it wasn't something I was passionate about. I'd wake up in the morning and I'd be in a fucking foul mood for no reason. She'd ask me what was wrong and I'd tell her I was fine; it'd take her all day just to get out of me that I was in a shit mood and that I didn't know why. I noticed she'd have her girlfriends from footy over more and more, and some nights when I'd get home from work, I felt like I wasn't wanted in my own home. I loved hanging out with all the girls, too, but it was always just this underlying feeling I wasn't welcome. I don't think it was intentional on her part at all, but I do wonder if she had her friends over a lot to distract her from being alone with me and the kids because of the shit we were going through.

Just after we'd moved into a new house, it really hit home for me just how torn she was over where to go with our relationship. One night, we pulled up in the driveway and we were just sitting there in the car, talking about our relationship, and she broke down in tears.

'Look, I think you've just got to do this, Soph,' I told her. 'You've got to do it for us, I can't take any more of this back and forth.'

On the surface, there had been nothing wrong throughout all of 2018. We were still having sex with each other, and everything seemed almost normal. But something wasn't quite right.

'You've got an itch and you've got to scratch it,' I told her. 'Whether this is something casual that you explore every now and then, or whether you are now gay, you have to find that out for yourself. But more importantly, you have to find that out for us – because what do we do? Do we stay married but more openly, and this is something you casually tap into? Or is it the end for us; do we separate? Whether it's a phase or it's you for life, you have to do this for your sake and for our sake – and whatever happens, I'll be here you.'

Sophie has said to me multiple times that I didn't have to be so supportive of her exploring when we separated. And I guess she's right, I could have gone either way with how I reacted. I could have been a real prick about it. But I have too much respect for her as the mother of my children and as a woman to not help her and support her. Because me being a prick and storming out, being an egotistical male, wasn't going to help the situation, and at the end of the day, I was never in the dark about anything, and I respect Soph for that. I'm not in the dark about her life now, either, because I'm a first point of call when she needs someone to talk to. She knows she can trust me, and I know I can trust her. But after she'd hooked up with another woman a few times, I think she started to feel guilty about the whole situation, and that's what led to the breakdown that night in the car.

As happy as I was to support her, I was still not doing well mentally, dealing with my own lack of purpose in life. Soph knew I was struggling, but I never told her how bad it got – that it got to the point where I thought about taking my own life. It was always the thought of my kids that kept me going, because I love being a dad so much. But the hatred I had for myself when I looked in the mirror . . . I couldn't stand the person I saw looking back at me.

Soph and I were still living together at this stage, which was hard because she was on such a high. Yes, she was going through a lot of her own transitions, but she was on this incredible trajectory with what she wanted in life and in her career. Meanwhile, I was caught in a downward spiral.

Even though we hadn't completely called time on our marriage yet, there were times I could see clearly that it was ending. In Easter 2019, we went away for a weekend to a friend's place in Torquay and the girl Soph was seeing came, too, and that did hurt a bit. I was in one room with the kids while Soph was two doors down with her new partner, and even though she'd pulled me aside to discuss the sleeping arrangements and we'd come to that decision together, it was still a bit tough for me. It was the right thing to do – Soph was seeing someone, I wasn't going to make her stay in a room with me and have the person she was seeing sleep by themselves – but it was a strange situation and reflecting on that weekend now, I probably shouldn't have gone.

Soph was always checking in and making sure I was okay with everything, too – it wasn't one quick conversation, it was an ongoing discussion between us. If we ever felt uncomfortable or as if we needed to say something, we could. We always communicated everything really well and it wasn't like I was sitting around miserable, or always at home with the kids while she was out living her best life. She gave me ample opportunity to go out but where I was at in my life at that stage, I didn't want to.

My biggest problem was that I didn't let her in enough to how I was really feeling sometimes. I often put up a wall and said I was fine when I should've given more of an indication of what was going on with me. But I was brought up never to sook, never to complain – just put everything aside and get on with things – so sometimes when I express my emotions, I feel like I'm having a whinge.

I did open up a bit on that weekend away, though.

Soph and our friend sat me down and asked me what was wrong, and I remember crying, telling them that I would wake up in the morning in what I called 'rages'. I had all this pent-up anger inside of me that I didn't know how to release. I remember saying to them that I would sometimes sit in my car and want to go head-on into a tree, because I didn't know how to express what I had inside me.

It got to the point where I needed us to make a decision. 'Soph, we've got to announce we're separating. We just have to get it out there.' I know she was hesitant, but as long as we were under the same roof, still a 'happily married couple', according to the public, I couldn't pursue my own happiness. She would tell me I needed to get out there, have some fun, have sex with someone, but I couldn't. The reality of it is, I was one of the most recognisable husbands in Melbourne thanks to our social media profile. So if I went out to a nightclub and tried to pick someone up, people were going to see me and think, 'What the fuck? He's married with two kids!'

I explained that to Sophie, and she understood. I was living in a house where her needs were being fulfilled – and I was genuinely happy that was happening for her – but mine weren't. For my sake, we needed to announce that we were separating. Once we did, I started to feel better about myself in terms of where I wanted to go and I'm in a much better place now. I'm much more at peace and I believe I'm now starting my journey to find myself – I'm finally doing what Soph was doing three years ago. I've gone through all the shit and I'm now starting to come out the other side with some clarity around where I want to take my life and my career.

What I never told Sophie is that her journey and everything she went through inspired me to go and find my own direction. She helped me sit back and realise that we actually weren't happy. I wasn't happy. I was acting like a miserable sack of shit because I thought I had to live this life according to someone else's rule book; a life of just work, come home, try to be the best husband, go to work again, come home . . . on repeat forever.

But then, there was her – pushing boundaries to find her true happiness and making me ask myself, 'Well, why can't I do that, too?'

Chapter 1

I was running late. Again.

At almost 30, you'd think I'd have learnt by now how to manage my time a little better . . . But no, I still insisted on challenging myself to get anywhere and everywhere in the shortest amount of time possible.

Sigh.

Only eight weeks earlier, I'd given birth to my second baby – my daughter, Florence – and I was on my way to one of my first 'working' events since she'd arrived, as a guest speaker on an AFL panel. (I've always worked hard, but let me tell you, dolling yourself up for a guest speaking appearance while you still have stitches in your fanny was new territory for me.) It was early 2017, the league's inaugural season was about to kick off and I'd been invited to speak because I'd grown up in a pretty well-known footy family, the Shaw family, and am a vocal advocate for female representation in sport. My dad had always worked in the AFL professionally – as both a player and coach with Fitzroy, Essendon and Adelaide Football Clubs, as well in senior management at Fremantle FC – so I basically grew up in footy changerooms around the country. Plus, I had married an AFL player. I had lived and breathed the game at every stage of my life, so it made a lot of sense that I was so passionate about it.

I know the game, I love the game, and I was absolutely stoked when the AFLW started up. I'd taken Floss to the first ever AFLW game when she was ten days old, which was such an emotional night for me as both a woman and a mother. Sure, I think the hormones were still raging through my body, but it was also such a significant, huge moment in history both for females and the future of our position in sport – and the fact that I got to be there with my daughter to witness it was really special.

So, there I was, racing to speak for an audience, the sweat dripping from under my milk-filled udders running down my stomach and soaking into the post-natal recovery shorts I'd decided to squeeze on underneath my leather skirt. Whose brilliant idea was that?

I raced into the hotel where the panel was being held, ran into the lift and pressed the button . . . wrong floor, of course.

Fuck. I was a sweaty mess and so nervous about getting up on stage – not because of any fear of speaking; more so because I was still in post-partum haze and, I reiterate, the under-boob sweat was real. (It's an issue on any given day with size 12GG boobs but add two proverbial gigantic hot water bottles on your chest thanks to your now 14-I-cup breastfeeding boobies and, woah, its wet 'n' wild under your shirt.)

As a company director, digital marketer, social media influencer and the owner of multiple businesses, I hold myself to a high standard when it comes to work events (speaking events in particular), and I strive to be the consummate professional. My personal presentation is so important to me, so I like to always source and style myself, as well as making sure that my prepared talk is in immaculate condition. I am a 'cram under pressure' type of gal and it's always worked for me. It's how I operated best throughout school, university and now for work, so in regard to my preparation ahead of speaking engagements, it's not uncommon to find me sitting up late at night, surrounded by pages and pages of handwritten notes (I've always retained information best by handwriting it), covering information on my expected talking points. I've also been known to stick notes up around my bathroom as a way of retaining information in order to present to the best of my capabilities.

As the elevator dinged to let me know I was at the right level, I could feel the panic rising.

Oh God, is my boob leaking?

I fumbled with my bag as the doors opened and I stepped through.

'Just in the green room to your right, Sophie,' a lovely staff member said as she ushered me towards a door. The tiny room was buzzing as the other women inside all chatted to each other. I didn't know who they all were at first, but the handful of girls wearing their club polos were obviously the footy players I'd be speaking alongside up on stage any minute.

When you're on a panel, it's pretty standard to be introduced to a whole lot of people all within the space of 60 seconds, and as I was taken around the room and introduced to football players, administrators, various volunteers and other people (whose roles I can't now recall), just remembering everyone's names was far too much to take in, given my newborn-induced sleep deprivation and the tizz I was in over being late. All I could think about was the moustache I hadn't had time to wax. Shit, have I got a sweat droplet hanging off my top lip? Ugh . . .

'Hi, I'm Sophie, nice to meet you!'

'Hi, yes, Sophie Cachia, so lovely to meet you.'

And so it went on . . .

Then there was her.

'Hi . . .'

My world froze.

When you hear about people throwing out phrases like 'the world stopped' or 'I saw stars', I always thought it sounded like a bit of bullshit. But as I shook this woman's hand, the electric current that ran between us was instantaneous. Energy ran between us – or perhaps just coming from my end. It was as close to an out-of-body experience as I could have ever imagined – and I'd never felt anything like it before in my life. Time stood completely still – and, yes, I am now one of those people who says that stars surrounded her in slow motion.

My mind was racing as she introduced herself.

Who is this woman?

I need to know her.

Oh my God, look at her arms . . . they're so . . . sexy.

She wasn't 'pretty'. Not in the traditional sense that I had been made to believe thanks to societal conditioning, anyway. During a discussion in late 2020 with my good friend Deni Todorović – a proud non-binary human and activist in the LGBTQIA+ community – we spoke about this concept. Once upon a time, we had both associated the word 'pretty' with femininity – a clear indication, we agreed, that we'd been taught to associate certain descriptive words with gender stereotypes. But this is a way of thinking from which we've since both evolved. It is important for me to note this as part of my story so that when I have 'labelled' or stereotyped, it's clear that these were the beliefs and thoughts of a past version of Sophie, not the evolution of her.

The woman who stood before me at the event was much shorter than me and very masculine in appearance. (Something else I have learnt over the past few years is that I'd instantly assumed her gender and pronouns based once again on societal conditioning, rather than asking her – though I now know how she identifies.) She had soft, beautiful skin that seemed to glow, yet had muscular arms and bulging veins from her fingertips to her biceps – something I'd never seen up close on a female before. Her eyes were piercing, sharp – the kind that look straight into your soul. I found myself inspecting her hands as she so firmly shook mine. They were strong, sturdy, with very short nails, bitten down to the bed. Protruding veins, as I'd so often seen on guys. 'Man hands', I called them. When she spoke, her voice was deeper than I expected. Even her scent was masculine, and it struck me that, physically, she possessed everything that I found attractive in my husband. She wore no makeup, her hair was thrown into a bun on top of her head . . . she was completely untouched.

So, whilst my then-conditioned brain hadn't labelled her as 'pretty', she was without a doubt the most strikingly beautiful person I had ever seen in my life. And it was in that moment my world changed forever.

I'd never felt this way about anyone before – so instantaneous – and certainly not about a woman. I'd always been able to appreciate another woman's physical beauty upon introduction, but this feeling was something new to me. This wasn't just me objectively taking in her looks. This was intense attraction – and I had never been physically attracted to a woman before in my life. So while one part of my brain was absolutely enraptured by this gorgeous, intriguing, powerfully sexy woman standing in front of me, shaking my hand, then the other half of me was thinking, What the fuck, Sophie? Why are you attracted to her? Why are you attracted to a woman?

I admit, I was really rattled after that. The next few moments were a blur as I went around the room chatting with the other people who would be speaking that day, prepping to get up on stage. But I kept looking over my shoulder.

Who is that woman? And why do I care?

I was married, after all, and still very much in love with my husband. We'd just had our second baby for God's sake. We were happy. I was happy! Our relationship was wonderful. Sure, there were a few issues, but nothing out of the ordinary, nothing that you wouldn't expect to see in any marriage at some point. In the eight years I'd been with Jaryd, my eyes had never found their way to anyone else – male or female – with this level of intensity, intrigue or sexual attraction.

Whatever had just passed between me and this woman, I was truly shaken and as the night wore on, I couldn't tear my eyes away from her, even as I was speaking. I couldn't stop staring at her nails. They were so different to my pink acrylic talons and I was surprised when I realised . . . I liked them. Usually I'd be thinking, 'Oh God, look at her fucking nails. What are you doing?' But I wasn't. I recognised she was different to me, to anything I'd ever been surrounded by . . . and I liked it. All I could think was how sexy those hands were; what they'd be able to do to me.

Listening to her talk later during breaks in the program, hearing snippets about her life and how passionate she was about female equality in sport, I soon found I was no longer just intrigued by her looks. I was quickly becoming interested in her as a person. She spoke so confidently, so assuredly, and with such passion about footy – something that I loved so much, too. I was so absorbed in her stories about her life, her time in the sport, what it meant to her to be there that night, and I could see that there was, in fact, more to her than moisturised biceps and intoxicating eyes. She was really intelligent, empowering, and – most appealing to me – she was really interesting. I had to get to know her.

As the night wrapped up, we all stood around mingling for a while, and I wasn't surprised at this point to discover I was totally giddy around her. We were all standing around talking as a group, but I was completely fixated on this woman. I was surprised to realise, though, that she seemed to be interested in me as well – not completely besotted in the way that I was with her, but there was something there drawing her to me.

She admitted that she'd had no idea who I was before the event but had Googled me and seen that I had 200,000 Instagram followers — she looked impressed. I've always found it quite hilarious when people I've met have warranted me some 'celebrity status' because of the number count on my followers list. Even elite athletes or famous Australian actors have done this, when in fact it's me standing there jaw-to-floor over them. They are the professionals, they are the 'real deal' — they are the famous ones here who deserve recognition and notoriety. Despite what some people would like to believe, Instagram followers have never been significant to me. Sure, for my career they are — in my role on social media, I am paid purely based on statistics, market reach, ROI, traction, targeting set audiences, etc. But some live with the narrative that just because we 'work' on social media, that we 'live' by social media — and for me that's far from the truth.

The more we chatted amongst the crowd, the more I got the sense that I, too, had intrigued this woman. So, we followed each other on Instagram, exchanged a few details, and made plans to catch up. After what I didn't realise at the time would be a life-changing meeting, I got in an Uber and I went home to my husband and my two babies. I had no idea what my feelings meant at that point — the confusion left me in a silent stare out of my window. All I knew was that I needed to know more.

~

As my Uber wove through the streets away from *her,* taking me further and further from the fantasy and back to my life, I scrolled through the photos I'd had taken on the night with various people at the event – including her. *'Gosh, I look so bad,'* I thought. Never mind the fact that I'd birthed my second baby just a few weeks earlier, I still judged myself harshly based on the possible perception of me she might be left with. Always a naturally confident person – one who has been blessed with quite a positive outlook on my physical appearance – I suddenly hated that photo. I hated that she might see it later and think I wasn't perhaps as appealing as she'd remembered. I didn't care if it was on social media for the world to see; I cared what *she* was going to think, that *she* would think I looked bad.

I walked in the front door, bursting to tell Jaryd about the night. 'You would not believe what just happened to me,' I laughed, setting my bag down on the kitchen table as I filled him in. 'I just had my *moment.'* Jaryd and I had talked about these 'moments' in the past – you know, the love-at-first-sight moments, those people who swear they met someone and fell instantly in love. I was previously a bit judgmental about it the idea of a 'moment', I'll admit, based on the fact I'd always believed love and attraction went far deeper than purely looks. I'd always found myself attracted to and more inclined to get to know someone based on a soul connection and if their personality could make me laugh.

But if it wasn't love at first sight – what was it? All I knew was that this was my first encounter of a 'moment'.

'I just met this girl,' I giggled to Jaryd, 'this woman . . . and I think I've got a crush on her. I think I just had my moment.'

It was normal for Jaryd and I to be so blatantly open with each other. If a beautiful woman walked past us in the supermarket, I would watch Jaryd look at her and giggle. Jealously was never, ever a trait of mine in that relationship. We understood each other on such a deep-rooted level, and with such open communication at all times comes great trust and respect. I was completely transparent with him about the night and how things had played out, my feelings I'd felt through both my mind and my body.

But I didn't like girls! I was married . . . to a man. I'd only ever dated men. I'd only ever had sexual experiences with men! My confusion was obvious as I explained to Jaryd in detail my attraction towards her arms and hands, her deep voice, and the way she spoke about playing footy like Jaryd would. Yet, she was a *girl*, with boobs and a vagina. What the fuck?! We were both in hysterics when I proclaimed, 'Jaryd – she even gave me fanny flutters!'

After an intense conversation about her, we headed to bed as usual, neither of us having any idea that this conversation would lead to us spending the next few years navigating our entire relationship – although much, much later, Jaryd confessed to me that he'd seen a spark in me that night that

11

he'd never witnessed before, and he knew nothing would ever be the same again.

~

When I tell you it was a slow burn from there, I mean it was s-l-o-o-o-w. It might've been an instant attraction for me, but there was a lot to process. This woman and I became friendly on Instagram, commenting on each other's posts, replying to each other's stories – but it was nothing, right? Just some schoolgirl crush that I would giggle about over cocktails with my friends. 'Oh, Jesus,' my best friend joked. 'You watch all of us start finally settling down at 30 and you'll be going through a mid-life crisis, getting divorced and becoming a lesbian.' I couldn't have predicted that that joke would become a reality.

I didn't know if she was seeing anyone, if she might have a boyfriend, or if she could possibly be gay. Looking back now, it's obvious to me where she was at in her life, but at the time I was totally naive to this unexplored world. I soon became obsessed with finding out if she had a partner. Why did I care, though? I was happily married. To a man! Remember, Sophie? I didn't even like girls, right? Yet here I was, so heavily invested into a life I shouldn't have cared about.

As I dived deep on her Insta page, scrolling back through photos, treading dangerously in that 'you've-scrolled-back-to-2016-please-don't-accidentally-like-a-photo' territory, I noticed she had a few snaps with this one particular girl but I was at a loss to find the concrete evidence I needed. No lovey-dovey captions that I was renowned for spurting to the internet, no obvious displays of affection in the pictures, not even a glimpse of a love emoji to seal the deal.

Maybe they're just housemates, I reasoned. *It could be her best friend.*

What an idiot.

My stomach knotted up and I got butterflies every time she'd message me, and even though our interactions didn't feel flirty, I *wanted* to flirt with this woman. I was getting a kick out of her; I'd get excited when my phone would light up and I'd see her name on my screen. Jaryd was across all of this, mind you, and I cannot stress that enough. This wasn't some top-secret operation, an illicit emotional affair, or a devious plot I had concocted behind his back. I read him every single message we would send each other, and it became almost a little joke between us, him laughing at how giddy I was when she'd text but then going on to help me draft a response. Looking back, I can't figure out if I was at the point of even understanding what was actually happening here, or if I was simply in denial. Because whilst it was a bit of fun for me, it was never something I would've even considered acting on back then. I was married. I thought I was happy. Jaryd was great. I was just having some harmless fun.

Finally, I got it out of her: yes, she had a girlfriend; yes, it was that woman in the pictures on her Instagram; and yes, they'd been together for a few years. I respected that, and almost found it a relief. Was she now off-limits to me? Not because I was in a committed marriage, mind you, but because *she* had a partner. It did give me a slight wake-up call – a bit of a dog-shaking-the-water-off-its-fur moment – but somehow, no matter how dry I thought I was, I was leaving a trail of wet footprints behind me.

She still held so much *intrigue* for me. Did I ever consider acting on it? Absolutely not, and not because I wasn't 'allowed' to. Freedom to experiment was on the table within our relationship – not constantly – but if a fun sexual experience arose, we would always discuss it with an open mind. It was being with a *woman* that was not a possibility for me. The thought just didn't make sense to me, despite how much it appeared my body was starting to crave it. 'Nope, she's a cool chick, we're going to be great friends,' my logical brain would tell itself. 'But those hands . . . those fingers . . . what would they feel like . . . inside of me?' It was not even something I allowed my brain to consciously consider, and I thought that if I didn't give my attraction to this woman the credit that it really deserved, then maybe it wouldn't be real.

So, I tried to forget it. I tried to forget her.

But I couldn't. I so desperately wanted to know her, to be a part of her life. 'Was this really *her*, though?' I would ask myself.

Or was it that this fantasy was providing me with something I was lacking in my real life?

I got my chance to see her again a couple of months later. I'd been invited to a charity walk, Move In May, which is run by Stand Up Events – an organisation that delivers programs to create safe and inclusive environments for everyone whilst fighting sexual and gender discrimination in sport. Founder Angie Greene has not only become a good friend of mine over the years, but she's also played an integral role in my education across the LGBTQIA+ space and I am forever grateful to be an ally alongside her.

I was going to be attending with my family – my husband, my son and my daughter – and you'd best believe that I was counting down the days. I was so excited that I'd be seeing her again, this woman I hadn't been able to get off my mind since that first meeting.

Oh my God, I'm going to see her again.

Oh shit . . . I'm going to see her again!

What should I wear?

How do I do my hair?

I wanted to look . . . good. For her.

What is actually going on with me here?

I'd always loved being sexy for my husband. I loved nothing more than when I'd be in the bathroom getting ready for a night out, or an event, and he'd come in and say, 'Oh fuck, you look amazing.' My entire life, I'd never dressed for anyone except for myself – until I met Jaryd. He always looked at me with such admiration, no matter what I looked like, but it was nice to see his face when I'd dressed up and made an effort. I didn't ever care what anyone else thought; I'm always confident in how I dress, I always love what I wear and I feel good in it. But if I was out to impress someone else, it was Jaryd and Jaryd only. I wanted to look good for my man, you know?

Yet suddenly, here I was wanting to look good for someone else. For *her*. It was now *her* that I wanted to make think, 'Wow,' when I walked in, even though the reality was I was only going to be wearing active wear since we were partaking in a 4km walk. Still, I fake tanned the night before and I carefully stuck on false eyelashes with expert precision the morning of the walk (because, of course, fake eyelashes and some terribly bad fake-tanned hands were going to make this woman fall head over heels in love with me).

I was nervous, so nervous, that I was going to see . . . her.

Sophie, what the fuck?

Why do you feel like this?

Clearly, what I was feeling was more than 'just friends', but while I was inching towards admitting that to myself, part of my brain just wouldn't fully accept it. I didn't have any intentions of cheating on my husband, but that wasn't even the biggest factor standing in the way. It was simply . . .

I'm not gay. I'm not bisexual. I'm not.

Being with a woman didn't even occur to me as an option, which sounds crazy now, but in terms of my upbringing, the way I grew up, I wasn't surrounded by gay women. I had never seen that side to life. To me, you found a man – a man, specifically – you got married, you had babies, you got a cute house with a nice white picket fence . . . it was the suburban dream, and it was the only option I thought I had, the option that had been ingrained into me since early childhood. I wasn't against same-sex relationships at all, of course, it just wasn't something I'd ever considered to be part of my journey, or an idea I'd explored for myself. So, for anyone who has been through – or is currently facing a similar identity crisis as this – you can imagine both the shock and the internal struggle I began to process as the realisation dawned on me that I had actual *feelings* for 'her'.

We arrived at the charity walk and I quickly found her amongst the crowd. She introduced me to her friends – mostly footy players and other women with their female partners – and again, I was instantly intrigued. These people were so wildly different to all the women I knew, the girls I'd grown up with and the social circles with which I regularly associated. They had such a naturally warm, welcoming vibe about them – a safe space, I felt – and they were all so unique and confident in their individuality. No one cared who I was or what I did – I was simply a friend of a friend and that was enough for me to be instantly accepted by the group with open arms. As we all got to know each other, and they handed my gorgeous baby daughter around for selfies, I observed this woman within her natural habitat. What was it about her and this group that made me feel like I, too, wanted to be here? Still, it would be another whole year before I began to pay any real attention to the feelings that she'd stirred up inside of me since our first meeting.

We stayed chatty on Instagram, but to be honest, I don't think I could call us actual 'friends' at that stage. I'd go to watch her games when I had time, and I was starting to become mates with people in her circle. But the whole time, despite many hot and cold attempts at shutting it down, I still had this hidden crush, this obsession, this fascination smouldering away in the back of my mind.

I assume that a conservative straight thinker would approach this situation with a completely different mindset than I did, and I'm sure there will be many readers here with frustration that I didn't pay attention to the red flags waving dramatically in front of my face at this point. I was constantly fighting my intense attraction to her, and I'd go in waves of shutting it down fiercely to focus on my life as a married woman and mother of two. But my true spirit kept reminding me that I was entitled to wonder, to dream, to allow my intrigue to run free.

The internal struggle is something I probably haven't spoken about to many people aside from Jaryd and my best friend. Never family, never online. The reality was that I didn't even know what was happening to me, and that's why when people asked for answers, I didn't have any to give. So many times I truly thought it would all go away; that perhaps my marriage had hit a few hiccups thanks to recurring issues that I couldn't see changing, and that I was just taking this opportunity to distract my mind temporarily. But deep down, that was the mind of a society-trained young woman, and not the real Sophie. The true Sophie goes off the power of intuition, passionate love and emotion, and a constant yearning for more in this thing we call life.

Chapter 2

As the youngest of four girls, I've always been the baby of the family. My twin sisters are in the middle – they're two years older than me – and then there's my eldest sister, who's seven years older than me. As far back as my memory can take me, Mum stayed home with us and she was definitely dedicated to our home life – running a tight ship, a hot dinner on the table every night at 6.30pm while we watched the Australian classic, *Neighbours*.

My dad worked in AFL footy, so he was away a lot for work ever since I was very young. I always thought it was a really cool job, and with most of my childhood spent growing up in Melbourne – the heart of AFL – so did a lot of people around me. It was because of Dad's job that I had quite a unique childhood – one that took me to some interesting places, and one that took myself and my family through both light and dark times. Dad worked as the senior coach at Fitzroy from 1991 to 1994, Adelaide Footy Club from 1995 to 1996, and was an assistant coach at Essendon Football Club from 1999 to 2005, alongside Kevin Sheedy. The Bombers won the premiership in 2000, too, so I got to experience some things that fellow AFL superfans could only dream of. Riding in players' cars for the Grand Final Parade (typical young Sophie, waving to the crowd like she had some sort of significance), having the Windy Hill security code so I could walk in and out of the club as a ten-year-old to go see Dad and the players (Essendon was renowned for being a very open, family club), and having AFL greats like James Hird, Matthew Lloyd and the Johnson brothers over for dinner every week. Tuesday dinners were the norm for us, and back then, that was a huge flex. All the boys at school were in awe when I'd tell them who was coming around that night.

'Aww, Soph, seriously? Can we come?!'

Only occasionally would Mum let me bring just *one* of the boys, so they'd battle for the spot. I felt like the coolest kid in school.

But it wasn't always that way. When Dad was senior coaching at Adelaide, that was a really tough time for all of us as a family, and looking back now, I believe it significantly shaped me into the person I am now as an adult. I get

21

extremely emotional when I revisit this part of my life, despite some of the memories being hazy – the emotion and pain in my chest are forever fresh.

I was four years old when we moved to South Australia for my dad to take up the biggest role in sport in the state at the time. At that stage, Port Adelaide didn't yet exist – so Adelaide – with its small-town vibe – was heavily focused on the Adelaide Crows. And Jesus-fucking-Christ, were they *hardcore*. When the team wasn't performing well, the entire City of Adelaide turned against my dad. Because in sport, if a team isn't performing, the coach must cop all of the blame – right?

Well . . . not all of it. His kids and wife had to cop some of that shit, too.

My sisters and I were just little kids when all of this was going on. We didn't understand the extent of the hatred being directed at my dad, at the whole family. My older twin sisters and I would race to the front door on the morning of a game day to count how many eggshells we could find all over the front of our house and in the garden. It was a fun game we liked to play – we were so innocent to the malicious acts that had occurred during the night. My older sister tells a story of being eleven years old at the local Semaphore Blockbuster getting a Friday night video when Dad was approached by a disgruntled Crows fan, who politely told Dad – in front of his daughter – how shit he was and that he needed to, 'Fuck off back to Victoria.' Dad, who never usually reacted in these situations, furiously chased this man out of the store. He was always brave enough to put on a front for himself, but he was – and, to this day, still is – a fierce protector of his girls.

My poor mum was ostracised in our own neighbourhood. No-one at the footy club wanted to be friends with the coach's wife if the team wasn't winning. She had one friend – Leanne – who she'd met through my sister's netball club. Leanne is still one of my mum's best friends today and is someone I consider family – a true sign of loyalty and a genuine adult friendship that I can now appreciate as an adult myself. There would be journalists out the front of the house, bashing on the door, pushing it open and shoving cameras in my mum's face. Towards the end, we even had a security guard who would sit out the front of our house in his car 24/7, just making sure we were all safe – not that me or my sisters had a clue why he was there. We just thought he was a family friend that we'd wave to on the way to school.

I saw my mum cry a lot, but I never understood why. I remember seeing her out in the driveway on her hands and knees, still in her dressing gown – so early it was still dark – scrubbing my dad's car on game day because it'd been vandalised.

'Mum, what are you doing?'

She'd shoo me away, telling me to hurry back inside – I now know it was because she didn't want Dad to know about it. In a sense, I consider myself quite lucky that I was too young then to comprehend what was actually going on, because looking back now – as a devoted mum to Bobby and Floss, and as a partner – it must have been horrific for both of my parents to experience this but to have to stay strong, not just for each other but for their four children who they'd packed up and moved interstate. For my dad, seeing what his family was being put through simply because of his job, but also for my mum, because she could see her husband out there busting his ass in a very public job to provide a life for the family . . . only to be humiliated and hung at the cross for a public stoning every weekend.

My sisters and I were also severely bullied thanks to the footy team's failings. I have raw memories of screaming, crying, refusing to go to school, and my mum – who was obviously upset, too – having to literally drag me to the car, shut me in and lock the door just to get me there. I'd wake up in the morning pretending to be sick, too, in the hope I wouldn't be sent. I'd cry and beg Mum to believe me, racking my brains for yet another excuse that might mean I could stay home. I must've been in prep or kindy at the time, and what breaks my heart the most is that, while I don't remember a lot around the specific reason I so desperately didn't want to be there, I do remember the feeling, the emotion, the desperation of wanting to be anywhere but at school. I was five years old.

'Please don't make me go, Mummy.'

There is one moment I do recall very clearly, though.

I was five, just one year older than my daughter is now, and I was out on the oval – it must have been lunchtime. I was on my own, as usual, as I didn't have any friends. Similar to Mum, everyone had ostracised me and my sisters long ago because Adelaide was losing and, obviously, it was our dad's fault.

The terror still haunts me as I sit here, 31 years of age, pounding heart, writing this. A group of Year Six boys came down to where I was sitting by myself and surrounded me, their shadows hanging over me blocking out the sun.

'Your dad's a loser!' they started shouting.

'Your dad's a dickhead!'

'My daddy says that we hate your daddy.'

I didn't get it. Why did they hate my dad? What did he do to them? Why had their parents told them to be mean to me? I stood up and tried to push my way past them, tears in my eyes and fumbling my snacks, but they were bigger than me and they were stronger than me. Twelve-year-old boys against a little five-year-old girl.

They wouldn't let me out of the circle they'd formed around me; they just keep pushing me until one shoved me to the ground. That's when it really began. They continued abusing me, they started throwing food at me, kicking me . . .

My twin sisters – who didn't have any friends either, but always had each other – saw what was happening from the other side of the oval and ran over. However, being aware of the danger, they stopped short of my group of tormentors. I remember reaching out to them, a hysterical five-year-old, literally putting my hand out for help from my only form of security in that moment, and they just stood there, fear written all over their faces, too. That fear in their eyes is something I will never forget, and the reason I understand why they didn't step in to help me. They stood helplessly, shaking their heads, petrified that if they tried to come forward and rescue their baby sister, the boys would hurt them, too.

All of this over a football game.

After some self-reflection, and quite some time spent with psychologists over the years, I can see how that period in time definitely shaped the person I am today. Whilst it's made me super resilient, unapologetic and proud of who I am at all times, it's also made for a very accepting, extremely understanding and non-judgemental adult Sophie. Even when people do horrible things, I can almost always find a way to see things from their point of view, or at least empathise with why they might've acted the way they did or said the things they said. I believe there's always a past reason for someone's actions against you.

And now, if a professional sporting coach is front-page news because they're getting mercilessly sacked, I always think of their families – the family that didn't choose to be put in the spotlight, but simply supported their loved ones.

They didn't ask to have the whole city, the state, even the whole country talking about them. Abusing them. Attacking them – emotionally and physically. I thank my lucky stars that I wasn't older and that social media was not yet in play. My resilience now allows me to live a public life online, immune to the vitriol and lies directed both towards and against me on a daily basis. But towards my loved ones? That's where I am my father's daughter. I am able to contain any form of reaction towards imbeciles online, but am simultaneously a fierce lioness protecting those in my pride at all times.

A coach might be a dickhead. Maybe they've made some horrible decisions throughout the season and, yeah, maybe their team sucks. But think of the kids at home who have to front up to school, and the wife whose name gets dragged through the mud. And don't you dare try to argue to me that 'that's why they signed up for'. No five-year-old girl deserves to be bashed at school because her dad's football team lost a fucking game.

Only recently, my sister messaged me about that incident in primary school, so many years ago.

'I've never forgotten that moment,' she wrote, 'and I live with so much guilt around it because I couldn't help my baby sister.'

Looking at my innocent children now, I can't imagine what I would do if something like that happened to them; and I can't imagine what it did to my parents, to my dad, knowing that his career dreams were shattering the lives of his family.

~

I always say I was Dad's 'boy experiment'. As the last of four girls, people would often joke with me that my dad was disappointed that he hadn't managed to have a son – and whilst he will vehemently deny any truth to it, there probably was a part of him that wished for a son, so I somehow became a stand in. One of my earliest memories with my dad is him teaching me how to kick a drop punt with an AFL footy. He taught me how to kick a torpedo too, and to use a speed ball. He put a cricket bat in my hand at three years old and I played my first game at five – receiving a hattrick on my first three balls in my opening over in Under 10 Boys. Fond memories surround family cricket games down in Bambra St, Lauderdale, where my older cousins would help me wrap my cricket ball with electrical tape to help me bowl a leg spinner to my wicketkeeper cousin behind the stumps. That cousin is former Australian Cricket Captain Tim Paine.

Everyone thought it was so cute back then, because girls 'didn't do' those sorts of things – so I was his token little boy. But while Dad was the one out with me in the yard, busy teaching me all the 'boy stuff', it was Mum I desperately wanted to impress.

With four kids, my household was extremely busy while I was growing up. I didn't have time to sook, cry or shout for attention, so I had to figure out very quickly how to just get on with things. I was independent from a young age with things like tying my shoes and dressing myself for school because Mum didn't have time to work her way down the queue to me. I often refer to my childhood as 'having to jump a little higher to be seen' in my house – not that I feel hard done by at all, but now, as an adult, I do crave a closer relationship with my mum. I've always yearned for that best friend relationship with her, probably because I didn't get a lot of one-on-one time with her as a kid.

I wasn't neglected in any way – not at all – but I do think my mum was so busy with everyone else (and, as I later learnt, trying to stay afloat in a high-pressure marriage), that when she saw I had been born a pretty confident, self-sufficient young girl, she devoted more attention to my sisters. It created a pattern for us that's persisted into my adulthood: she still thinks that I don't need her because, to this day, I am that strong-willed, independent, 'I'll be okay on my own' type of girl. But the truth is, I do need my mum. More than I've ever liked to admit. I really, truly do. In everything I did as a kid, and still in so much that I do now, it's all to make my mum proud of me, and I'm always waiting to hear those words. But I very rarely heard them.

This is where Mum and I are intrinsically different. I am a hyper-emotional communicator, whether good or bad. My mum, however, is a closed book to me. I know she is proud of me, even if she doesn't know how to say it – and I'm sure it will probably upset her to know how much it still kills me; that I am still that little girl, longing for those words. Somewhere inside, even at 31 years of age, I'm still the young girl yearning for Mummy to come give me a cuddle.

I don't recall growing up in a house where we said 'I love you' a lot, either. I know I *was* loved – my mum was (and still is) gentle and warm. She's very shy and reserved – again, the polar opposite to the woman I am now. Mum is someone who doesn't say much, but she will always share that her four beautiful girls are her greatest achievement in life.

My mum shows her love in other ways, and that's something I've come to understand more and more as I've grown older. That people *show love* in different ways and that we must accept emotions in diverse forms – even ones that are in contrast to how our own brains are wired. We all have unique attachment styles, distinctive love languages. My sisters and I have always said that Mum would never actually apologise if she'd upset us – I don't think I've ever heard the word 'sorry' come out of her mouth. But if any of us had had an argument with her in the morning, for instance, you'd get home from school and your whole bedroom would be clean, there'd be new sheets on the bed and there'd be a beautiful candle lit in your room. That's Mum's way, that's how she shows love – by doing things for others without words. To this day, I'll invite her over for dinner and she'll arrive and just start doing the washing or tidying the kids' rooms. I have to ask (or yell!) over and over for her to please just relax, sit down, and to let me cook for her.

It's just how she uniquely shows her love, but it is something I still struggle with. Sometimes I do just want to hear those words: 'I love you.'

(I loved a girl so desperately once, and upon reflection with my psychologist, I came to realise that it was because she treated me with the same somewhat tough love I felt my mum did. It was a very non-verbal, actions-over-communication type of love, and just like I have with my mum over the years, I spent *far too long* trying to change her, to get her to love me in the way I *wanted* to be loved – instead of simply accepting her way of offering it.)

My struggles came from not acknowledging the differences in how people convey love. I am loud, proud and expressive with my emotions, and I now overcompensate with my own kids to make up for the verbal validation I didn't receive as a child. I tell them 50,000 times a day, 'You are beautiful. You are great. I love you,' because I think children *need* to hear those things . . . I know I needed to hear them. When I'm telling Bobby and Florence how much I love them and how proud I am of them, I make them look deep into my eyes, so that I know they're listening and really absorbing what I am saying. As their mother, their nurturer and their safe place, it's crucial to me that they really comprehend how much I adore them and that it's embedded into their minds throughout adulthood that they were loved.

In fairness, Mum also finds my personality polarising at times. These days, when I try to talk to her about things that are negative or perhaps uncomfortable for her, she feels like I am on the attack and will walk away, avoiding any form of 'serious discussion'. Many introverts, I've discovered in life, will interpret such conversations as threatening and critical – whereas, to me, it's just an open discussion; an integral part of making my way through life. So I do find it sad that there are times I am simply trying to open up a dialogue, only to be ignored and criticised for 'attacking' people. I pride myself on my communication skills and letting people know how their actions make me feel – whether good or bad – but it's certainly a skill I've had to teach myself along the way, and something I still work at now. I have most certainly inherited my dad's temper and, at times, rage, and a confrontation is something I will never shy away from – but I suppose now, with maturity and having undergone an evolution into the woman I am today, I've also learnt to protect my energy and to be smarter with my battles. I think too many people mistake a calm, rational discussion – even one expressing a difference in opinion – for a verbal attack, and I believe it's their own insecurity that is creating that reality for them. A conversation might be uncomfortable or unpleasant to have, but that doesn't make it an argument. I see this a lot online as I regularly engage in open discussions with my followers about different viewpoints with an open mindset, but only when approached in a similarly respectful manner.

My mum has said to me on more than a few occasions, 'You think I'm not communicative, you should see what *my* mum was like!' – as if it's some sort of competition for who had it worse – and I do get a bit frustrated with her. If something her mother did hurt her, like a lack of communication or support, I've always questioned why she wouldn't try to break those patterns for her own kids. That's the exact reason I've chosen my parenting style to almost smother my children with an abundance of praise and love – to the point where they'll probably turn around one day and say, 'Mum, shut the fuck up, we get it, you love us!' I, alongside their dad, work very hard to make sure our home is an accepting, loving space with free-flowing conversation, where my children (and their friends) can come, knowing they can discuss anything without fear of judgement or discipline. Where they can feel safe in how they are processing something and will never be told their emotions are invalid – regardless of whether, as parents, we agree or disagree with the situation. To allow them as children, and as they transition into teens and then adults, to feel everything that they need to feel. I don't believe any experience should be shut off. I want my children to be exposed to as many emotions and situations as possible, so that, as they do evolve, they get to shape who they are themselves, instead of being moulded into what we as parents want them to be.

~

There was one moment with my mum, though, that I will always look to as a reminder of how much she loves me, and every time I recall this moment, I physically hold my open palms over my heart and my face beams with a smile.

When I gave birth to Bobby, I didn't want my mum in the room with me.

I'm 22, I'm independent, I'm having this baby with Jaryd, I'm an adult now . . .

But when it came to birthing Florence, all I wanted was Mum. I initially hadn't planned to have her there – it had never even occurred to me – it was going to be just Jaryd and me again, along with the student midwife I'd brought along for the journey. Yet, during my labour, I was suddenly overwhelmed with the idea that I needed a strong, female presence there in the room with me. Jaryd and I never found out what gender we were having before either labour, and throughout my second pregnancy I was convinced it was another boy. Hank, he would be called. Bobby and Hank Cachia. However, during my peaceful eight-hour labour at home, and into my active labour at the hospital, my intuition was speaking loudly to me, telling me it was going to be a girl.

A spur of the moment thought (amidst snippets of a gas-induced hallucination that I was Poppy from *Trolls* slip 'n' sliding down a rainbow) was that I needed my mum by my side. Immediately. Not to hold my hand, but to be a symbolic presence when I brought my baby girl into the world.

I was literally mid contraction when I grabbed Jaryd's arm. 'Get Mum, I want my mum.' I told him. We have a joke now that she must've been doing laps of the hospital in her car, because she was there in an instant, in typical Mum fashion – hair freshly blow-waved, gorgeous new Seed shirt on, like she'd been waiting for that exact call.

Mum immediately changed that environment for me. I was instantly calm – further highlighting that, no matter where I believe I'm at in life and how much I've grown up, and despite the fact that we have butted heads so often throughout our lives, I will always feel at home with my mum. She didn't interfere – she did just enough to let me know she was right there with me. Without instruction, she opened the birth suite blinds, the beautiful evening sun beaming right onto all of us. It no longer felt so clinical and scary, the natural light and warmth symbolic of the beautiful little ray of sunshine that was about to greet us earthside.

After Florence (originally named Betty but later changed) was born and Mum had gone home, she sent me a text message and it's one I've cherished ever since.

'That was one of the most beautiful experiences of my life, to see my own baby girl birth her very own baby girl,' she wrote. 'It's something I'll never forget. I love you so much. And I'm so proud of you.'

Chapter 3

Despite the horror of the Adelaide years, Dad gave us a pretty blessed life – hanging out with AFL legends like Kevin Sheedy and his kids on the weekends, travelling with the team to interstate games, taking the 2000 premiership cup to school for show-and-tell . . . it definitely wasn't all bad. But we did travel a lot with his job, which meant moving house and changing schools often, so again, I had to learn to be very adaptable from a young age. We lived in Melbourne off and on, with stints in both Adelaide and Tasmania, too. My dad even went over to Perth for two years on his own in a General Manager role at Fremantle Football Club while I did my final years of high school in Melbourne.

High school, as we know, can be tough for so many reasons. I loved school, but I've had a wall up from a young age. At times, it was pretty fucking brutal, to be honest. I was one of the 'cool girls' (ew, I hate that phrase now), part of the 'in' crowd, but I was always the first to cop shit from other people. One of my best mates in Year Seven was this gorgeous girl. She had beautiful olive skin, she had big boobs already, and she'd had braces in primary school, so her teeth were impeccable by the time she reached Year Seven. A couple of teenage zits, but it was nothing – she was simply stunning, a Kourtney Kardashian-type vibe. We quickly became best friends, but I was her opposite. Pale, see-through skin, thick, bushy eyebrows, body covered in freckles. I didn't have pimples at that stage, however, I was really self-conscious about my freckles. I remember going to her one day to seek some reassurance.

'Do you reckon my freckles are that bad?' I asked her one afternoon in her bedroom, having swiped on thick layers of Maybelline Mousse Foundation in an attempt to disguise the spots. 'I can cover them if they're really that bad.'

She shot me a look.

'I'd much rather have pimples than freckles. At least you can get rid of pimples.'

It might not seem that big a deal to some, but as a twelve-year-old girl, hitting puberty, wanting my friends' approval and support, it was a horrible thing to hear. I interpreted her words as something more along the lines of, 'Your face is ugly and you can't change it.'

That wasn't the first time I felt unsupported by my social circle. A year earlier, in Year Six, my group came up to me one day and announced that they didn't want to be my friends anymore, and I was banished from playing with them in the yard. People who know me best now know that I take responsibility for my shit, as I am far from perfect. I am the first to stand up and accept responsibility for anything I've done wrong to someone or in times I've upset them. This goes back to my belief in the power of open communication. But this time around, nothing had prompted it. They just stopped talking to me, out of the blue, without warning. I didn't get the opportunity to fight my case in the lunch break. We never spoke again.

It's a theme I saw repeated in high school, and one that continued well into my early adult years. For the longest time, I've tried to look inside – from an unbiased viewpoint – to figure out where I was messing up, why people I believe I loved and cared for so much seemed to be turning away from me. I always figured that, if everyone else thought I was the problem, then I must be.

What am I doing wrong?

Situations like that also really shaped a huge part of my life. It killed me at the time when people would behave that way, but it certainly made stronger because I had no option but to cop it on the chin and learn to back myself. It took me a really long time to realise that sometimes people treat you like shit because they're intimidated by you, by your choices in life. I think the confidence I've maintained in situations where society has told women to sit the fuck down for so long has been intimidating for some people I've known in my life.

My tendency to stand up for the little guy, as well as being brave enough to form my own opinions in the face of fixed mindsets, has also got me in trouble growing up. I have always been quick to challenge people's actions if I didn't think they were right or fair, and it never sat well with me when my high school peers would be so judgemental of choices that were counter to what they would do.

I'm sure we can all recall moments sitting around with friends at lunch at high school, talking about classmates, commenting on what someone was wearing on the weekend or who they were dating. For me, even if I didn't know them, or they were in the group of girls who I wasn't 'supposed to' like, I would refuse to comment or try to steer the conversation in another direction.

'Who cares?' I'd ask. 'That's her business. It doesn't impact us.'

Unfortunately, holding people accountable for poor comments in moments like these often makes them feel very uncomfortable, and I came to learn that when I've challenged others' way of thinking throughout my life, it can lead my being labelled as 'problematic'. Imagine being the girl in a cliquey high school group – an environment in which teenage girls are constantly seeking acceptance and approval from their peers – and choosing to go against the grain; having the confidence to stand alone, to form my own opinions and beliefs, at the risk of not 'fitting in' with the crowd.

I would always ask, 'Does that really matter to us, though?'

'Why does that bother you so much if they do that?'

'Why do you care what car she drives?'

Trivial matters, really. But the topics themselves weren't the point of the issue. The problem was that I was, and always have been, okay to run my own race, even if it meant I was disliked.

What other people were doing truly never worried me. If it didn't affect my life, why would I give it energy and attention? So at fourteen, seventeen, 25 . . . I was making some acquaintances reflect on their actions – and I don't think that felt good for them. I was branded 'difficult'.

Ironic now, really, that I work in a world where I face people like this every day. Commenting, criticising, forming opinions on my life, what I'm doing, what I'm wearing, who I'm dating . . . despite it having zero effect on their own lives.

I reflected on it a lot over the years until I finally realised that my presence, my very being, makes people feel uncomfortable. It's not intentional, of course, but my confidence, my approach to life and my willingness to call others out on their bullshit – and to call myself out when I need to – that scares people.

I am constantly asking myself: How can I be better? How can I do better? How can I be a better friend? A better partner? A better colleague? I'm always looking for ways to improve as a human and I think that can make a lot of people uneasy because it forces them to look at themselves, too. It forces them to face some potentially grim truths about themselves, and they can uncover parts of their own personalities they don't like so much.

I am not fucking perfect. I make terrible choices at times. I've treated people horribly at times in my life, and I've certainly done and said many things that I am not proud of. Things I am mortified to have done, really. But what I am proud of is that I accept my faults, I own who I am, and I live with the truth that we can all be better in terms of who we are inside. We all have that choice.

~

I went to the local co-ed school from Years Seven to Ten, but I moved to a renowned private school in Year Eleven to undertake my VCE. My parents sacrificed a lot so I could attend what was then a $14,000 a year school (now it sits around $30,000 per year, I believe). I'm very grateful for that opportunity now because I did do really well there, both in sport and academically, and I ended up getting fantastic marks that saw me accepted into Melbourne University. Yet, being a student at those two wildly different schools also exposed me to two opposing sides to life.

The local public school I went to was fantastic, with a wide variety of both sporting and academic pathways available, and with students from myriad different socioeconomic backgrounds. But when I got to the private school – prestigious and highly renowned for its elite facilities, academic results and calibre of students – the differences in the educational hierarchy were highlighted for me as I saw an uglier side to life; a very judgmental, entitled mindset that seemed to come of being from higher up the socioeconomic food chain, so to speak.

To my eyes, it seemed nastiness was praised, even encouraged within the student groups. When I first started, there were girls who'd tell me, 'Oh thank *God* you're here and not at that school anymore', as if it was something to be ashamed of. Yet, my sisters had gone there. My mum worked there. My friends were still at that school, and I certainly had no ill will towards it.

I remember sitting around at lunchtime with the girls in Year Twelve, talking about what some of them were getting for their eighteenth birthdays.

'If I do not walk out the front of my house to find a red BMW with a bright pink bow on it, I will never speak to my dad again,' one said.

I couldn't believe this sense of entitlement from a seventeen-year-old. My parents had saved and scraped together every penny they could to send me to the school. My mum had sacrificed moving us all to Perth to be with Dad at his job in

Freo just so I could attend this school. Whilst Dad had worked great jobs and I think we were always comfortable financially, we certainly didn't come from money. Yes, we lived in a beautiful area, but my parents always bought the cheapest house in the nicest street. They always made sure we went on family holidays, and we never went without anything we needed, but the reality is that having four kids is expensive. We always needed four- or five-bedroom homes. We always needed big cars. So while it may've looked like we were really well-off, with me at a private school, we weren't rich. Mum and Dad always ensured that had whatever we needed to be our best – new netball runners, school books, stuff like that – but we certainly never expected cars for our birthdays, let alone latest model BMWs with pretty pink fucking bows.

What was great about that private school, though, was the incredible work ethic the teachers instilled in me. They taught me a lot about discipline, structure, hard work, basic respect and organisation, things that I'd never learnt at my previous school. There, my friends and I would spend our spare periods going to Maccas or sitting out on the oval tanning, while at my private school, spare periods were strictly study periods. We had to go to the library and do our homework in the dead silence, and I actually really loved that. I loved having the structure, the discipline and the pressure to perform well. Now, as an adult, I always do my best work in high-pressure environments.

And I did do well, finishing in the top eight per cent of my state's peers across most subjects. Whilst I do now believe that choice in schooling systems is going to be different for each individual human, I definitely thrived there. I got to see that if you put in the effort, you can achieve great things. However, I also learnt that success can turn you into a very ugly person.

Experiencing both sides of the education landscape further shaped who I am today because I saw how hard I wanted to work; how hard I could work and how successful I could be when I applied myself, but I also learnt exactly who I *didn't* want to be. I never wanted to have that inflated sense of entitlement that some of my classmates had. I didn't want to have that gross outlook on life – that one's privilege reflected their worth – or to ever look down on other people because they didn't have the opportunities that I had.

Chapter 4

I don't have a lot of regrets in my life – I don't believe that you should regret things because, at the time it's exactly what you wanted. But there is one thing I look back on from my high school years that I wish I'd done very differently.

I was very into sport at a young age, and I was pretty naturally talented, too. My sisters and I all played a bit of netball, did some athletics at school, but I was innately gifted and I probably didn't realise just how good I was at the time. I was always taller than average, which was handy for sport, and by the time I was twelve I was regularly attending state championships in athletics (sprinting, triple jump and shotput) and also representing my home state of Victoria in netball at a national level.

When I was fourteen, I was in the middle of a game when my knee suddenly popped and blinding pain shot through my leg. It felt as if someone had held a shotgun to my knee and pulled the trigger, my kneecap exploding, shattering into a million pieces. I let out a horrific scream as I dropped to the cold ground of the outdoor court.

My mum and my coach bundled me up and half-carried me, a sobbing mess, to the physiotherapist at the Parkville State Netball Centre. Other parents from my team had also gathered, all of them unnervingly quiet. I didn't understand why they were acting as if somebody had died – the pain had eased by the time I was sitting on the physio's table.

I've just jarred my knee, what's the big deal?

'Guys, it's fine, it barely even hurts anymore,' I insisted, holding an ice pack to my injured knee, hoping that the events of the night would be dramatic enough to convince Mum to get me Maccas on the way home.

The physio asked me to point out where the pain was and to describe the noise I'd heard when it happened – a very clear and crisp popping sound, I'd told her – and the sombre mood only intensified. That sound, they explained, was a classic sign of a torn anterior cruciate ligament, and where I'd felt the pain was a good indicator that that was what had happened. The fact that my pain had subsided was also very textbook for a torn ACL.

My dad, who was coaching Essendon at the time, was interstate for a match the night it happened. I remember lying on the bed in the physio's room and Mum saying to me, 'Reidy wants to talk to you.' She was talking about Bruce Reid, the Essendon Football Club doctor, and I couldn't fathom why she'd called and bugged him on bloody match day. How embarrassing, Mum.

'What noise did it make?' he asked. 'Where did you feel it? Did it stop hurting ten minutes later?'

I answered all his questions and was surprised when he told me he was going to book me an immediate appointment and told me to give the phone back to Mum. After chatting with him a little longer, she hung up and told me that Reidy had said we needed to drive out to see another doctor, there and then.

'Mum! What the hell? I'm fine! Can we please just go home?'

No – apparently, we could not. After about a 50-minute drive, we arrived at the home of another doctor who was involved in the club, an older bloke who ushered us into his mansion of a home and sat me down on his bed. I was so fucking embarrassed – the poor man was in his dressing gown, his wife standing by in her slippers. We'd clearly inter-rupted them as they were getting ready to go to sleep.

'Seriously, why are we doing this? I am fine, I can walk . . .' At fourteen, I had no idea how serious a torn ACL was and

I was shocked when we eventually got back in the car and Mum told me I would need to have surgery.

'Soph, you're going to need a knee reconstruction. You're not going to be able to play netball for twelve months.'

What?

I almost laughed at her.

No, it doesn't even hurt . . .

I had just made the state Under 15s team, representing Victoria again, and the tournament was due to start in a couple of weeks. I'd spent months going through the gruelling try-out process and subsequent trainings camps – there was no way I could miss out on that! But when Mum did end up taking me to McDonald's on the way home, I knew something really was up. Mum *hated* McDonald's and we never ate it as kids, so when we pulled into the drive-thru, the severity of the situation began to sink in.

Within 48 hours, I was undergoing a full knee reconstruction on my right knee.

With the contacts we had through Dad's footy, I was put at the top of the list with Julian Feller, an internationally recognised Melbourne-based orthopaedic surgeon whose main area of interest was knee surgery. Julian was renowned for being the top surgeon to all the AFL boys when they needed operations. I didn't recognise at the time how lucky I was to have those sorts of privileges during my childhood – people can wait months simply to get an appointment with someone like Julian Feller and there I was, bumped to the top of his list, knee reconstruction done in record time, just like I was a professional player.

What I also didn't understand at the time was the recovery I was going to have to go through. At fourteen, I had absolutely zero concept of the emotional and physical battles I would face every day, nor could I have imagined the mental torture of having something I loved so much being so swiftly and completely taken from me.

That whole incident and the period of time that followed really did change my life, and while I wish I could say it was for the better, that injury and recovery process really threw me out mentally. My netball focus waned and I never quite got back to the level of potential I'd had before the injury, even though I did try, at times. I worked really hard with my dad, who put in so many hours to help me train and get my strength back. He was running with me down at the park, getting me access to the best rehabilitators, writing up his own programs for me, pinching me the top icing machines from the footy club – every advantage he could give me was mine when I needed it. But I was naive to how much I would actually have to work myself to get back to my best. While I was in rehab, I definitely took it all a bit for granted. I remember knowing I had youth on my side; I knew I was fit, I was naturally talented, I'd never had to put in much effort to be good at netball, or sport in general . . . I naively assumed – regardless of all of the professional advice I was given – that I'd be fine to carry on as I always had and would come back as strong as ever. What I quickly learnt was, natural talent aside, I wasn't resilient enough to put in the dedication that was required to come back from something like major knee surgery.

It kills me now, looking back, because I can see what my dad would've gone through, training alongside me; and my mum, who had dedicated so many trips to training sessions over the years – with nothing in it for her – watching her daughter, who had been born with such a gift, slowly letting it slip away.

~

I didn't stop playing altogether after I'd recovered from surgery, and I was still very good – I got back to playing state netball for Victoria at sixteen, and also played in the Championship League throughout my teenage years – which, back then, was one rung below the professionals. However, I always knew inside that I'd lost quite a bit of my motivation for the hard work, and as someone who was known for her leap as a defender, I knew I couldn't jump the same as I once had.

I was actually offered a full netball scholarship to attend the private school I moved to, but because my parents had already enrolled me years earlier, the school took that as 'proof' that they could afford to send me there, so the principal gave the scholarship to someone else. My first netball coach there was Eloise Southby-Halbish, the former Diamonds player, and she saw so much potential in me.

'You will play Centre for Australia one day,' she told me during a training session one night when I was in Year Eleven. (Despite being 'tall' in everyday life, I was 'short' in netball terms, so as I began playing at more elite levels, my natural key positions of Goal Keeper/Goal Shooter had to change, putting me in the midcourt.) Eloise had given me the greatest compliment. It was the highest praise from someone who'd represented Australia for many years, and someone who knew what it took to be the best. Still, I didn't commit myself the way I should have because, at that moment, Eloise believed in me more than I believed in myself.

My whole life, since I was six years old, had been dedicated to netball. At the age of thirteen, I was looking at three or four training sessions a week, games on Saturdays, interstate carnivals, training on Sundays, academy programs, rehab . . . you name it. And I think that when you get to sixteen or seventeen years old, that's when it's make or break as a professional athlete – and for me, I broke.

Not fulfilling my athletic potential with netball is, to date, my biggest regret in life. I live with guilt for the people that believed in me and who I subsequently let down. For my parents, who sacrificed time and energy to help me blossom as a highly skilled teenager, only to watch me throw it away.

I can look back confidently knowing I had the skill, and I'm at peace with that, but I'm also aware that professional athletes' success is just as much about their mindset as it is their physical ability – and I clearly didn't have the mental strength required to make it to the top back then.

I feared the negative too much after my surgery. I was scared of the hard rehab work and the disappointment I'd felt during the process. My playing style had changed after the operation, too, and I unfortunately allowed my ego to begin controlling my approach. I wasn't prepared to fail again, which, looking back, is piss weak. I was never 'bad', but now I was scared to be.

I let down everyone who had ever believed in me; but mostly, I let myself down.

When I watch the Australian Diamonds' games on TV now, I see girls on that team who I used to play with, and I think, 'That could've been me.' I think that's probably why I work so hard in other areas now to make something of myself, because I see so much wasted talent in that past life. I look back to a young girl who threw away a life that she would now love to be living.

Of course, on the other hand, my spiritual side allows me to believe that there is always a reason for everything. If I'd gone that way, I wouldn't have had my beautiful children so young, and being a mum is my favourite thing in the world.

But I won't ever let an opportunity pass me again. I don't want to live with that regret around anything else ever again, because I live with it every single day. I see these inspiring, strong netballers, and I know that could have been me. That could've been my reality, but I made the choice not to make that happen.

My career wasn't cut short because I wasn't good enough – I *was* good enough. But I made a bad decision. Everyone told me not to quit – the coaches and staff all told me not to throw in the towel – but I chose, and I chose wrong.

Now if an opportunity that comes my way interests me, I've promised myself that I will take it, even if it absolutely petrifies me. I no longer see fear and run from it. I look fear in the eyes, with my brain already working away in the background figuring how I'm going to burst right through it. I no longer see failing as something negative, but rather a crucial part of learning on your way to success.

Never fear failure. Fear the regret you will one day have for not even trying. Trust me.

Chapter 5

While I dated a couple of guys in high school, no-one compared to the amazing man I met when I was twenty: Jaryd Cachia.

Jaryd and I were always destined to meet. It was honestly too much of a coincidence *not* to be fate. I had just broken up with a boy who, looking back, was totally inappropriate. I laugh now, knowing exactly why my mum didn't think he was right for me. Parents are always right.

This guy broke up with me because he wanted to go out with the boys more, and I certainly wasn't cut up about it. I'm pretty sure Mum high-fived me.

After we split, I was invited by a girlfriend to a Tuesday night 'gathering' at the house of the guy she had been seeing.

A Tuesday night after we'd all finished working at the pub and I'd been at uni all day?

Absolutely not.

No. No!

But I felt bad letting her down. So what did I do? Thinking I was being so smart, I turned to the 'no' friend – you know, the pal that never wants to go anywhere or do anything, the girl who always says no. I told my mate that if our 'no' friend agreed to come, I would too. So when she said 'yes', it well and truly fucked up my plans.

And that's how I found myself heading to Ascot Vale at 10.30pm on a Tuesday night, going to God-knows-whose house, so my friend could hook up with her guy. Upon walking in, I realised this was much more than a gathering. The house was filled with men. Big, strong, wild men. Music was blaring, bodies were everywhere . . .

Where the hell am I?

I also quickly realised that we were the only three girls at the party. Ew. It wasn't until I noticed a quiet Eddie Betts, sitting with his feet up on the couch, tapping away on his phone, minding his own business, that it clicked: this was a 'football' party. An end-of-season party. A follow-on from the Mad Monday celebrations that had kicked off the day before.

Now, I was a football fan, yes – but these were not my people. These guys were Carlton. Ew, right? I was Essendon blood through and through, so other than the very renowned and popular Eddie, I couldn't have named one other player there.

Fast forward to later that night and I found myself chatting to a bunch of guys (as you do). One of them in particular stood out for his interest in conversation, his respectful manner, his eye contact whilst I spoke, which let me know he was really listening . . . and he had these drop-dead gorgeous blue eyes. He was charming – a year younger than me but worlds ahead in maturity compared to other boys I knew – and after spending the night in deep convo away from the group, we ended up sharing a kiss and a cuddle.

All of his qualities had already hit the pass mark for me, what really caught my attention happened at the end of the night, as my girlfriends and I were about to leave. He'd quietly asked for my number earlier in the night, away from the group, but as we went around the party saying our goodbyes to the stragglers before calling it a night, he realised he actually hadn't saved my number.

'Wait, wait, wait, Soph!' He burst into the room in a tizz. 'I didn't save your number – can you type it in again?'

The group of 'lads' burst into hysterics and he was aggressively heckled for what I can only assume was going against 'boy code' by showing genuine interest in a girl so openly in front of your teammates. It's widely known that footy teams are 'boys' clubs' and I'd seen a lot of it throughout my father's time working in sporting clubs. So whilst it shouldn't have been a big issue – you know, being the 'nice guy' – I knew that it was, in fact, brave of him to put himself out there so openly in that environment. It showed me he was a mature, genuine soul who was unapologetic for his interest in me.

When he asked me out for breakfast, I took it as another sign of his good character. An actual date from a nineteen-year-old! It was something I don't think my previous boyfriend had done in the almost two years we'd been together. Of course, I said 'yes', and he told me what time he would pick me up. When the morning arrived, as I stood behind my bedroom door rubbing what was left of my Sportsgirl Body Glow bronzer onto my legs, I heard a voice in my kitchen.

'Hello Mr Shaw, I'm Jaryd Cachia, nice to meet you.'

I froze.

What insanity is this?

What is this atrocity?!

What creature of this age doesn't just text when he's in my driveway, too petrified to come in and meet parents before a simple breakfast date?

That creature was Jaryd Cachia – and he had been raised by his parents to be a beautiful young gentleman.

Little did I know he had arrived early and was confident enough to knock on the door without telling me, introduce himself to both of my parents and stand in my kitchen chatting to them while I stood frozen, globs of body bronzer in my hands, one as-yet-untanned leg hoisted up on my desk, staring with shock at my door. My experience so far in life had led me to believe that this nineteen-year-old boy would text me a lazy 'Here' and that I should accept that as normal.

A teenage boy showing respect, and using manners and common decency?

What the fuck was this?

Early on in my relationship with Jaryd, I recall speaking to my mum about him while we had lunch together one day. Our relationship was still fresh, but he had slotted into my family so seamlessly, he instantly became a son to my mum.

'I don't care if you don't marry him one day, Sophie, but just make sure you have his babies,' she told me with a laugh. After all, she loved his striking blue husky eyes as much as I did (and yes, those babies we eventually had are both owners of the characteristic Cachia baby blues).

Jaryd broke up with me a couple of months later. I desperately wanted to grow up and play housewife. I think he had realised that he didn't want to be tied down at such a young age, and hey, upon reflection, I was probably 'a lot' for someone who'd never been in a relationship before! Us being so invested in each other's families so quickly was a bit too much for 'Cache', as he was known, who had always been infamous for his work with the women.

We split up only temporarily and it wasn't long before Jaryd and I were back on again and going strong – though I did have a one-night stand with another guy in our time apart.

With a friend of mine, actually – and it was spontaneous and fun, and it didn't mean a thing.

We're still friends to this day – not that I see him much now, but that's one thing about me – I've always been very capable of separating sex from emotion. I can be mates with anyone, even after they've seen me at my most vulnerable.

At the end of 2011, about twelve months after we'd first gotten together, Jaryd signed a contract to go play in the South Australian National Football League – the SANFL – in Adelaide. It was a decision I 100 per cent supported him on. Even though I was only 20, I wasn't really worried about my boyfriend living in another state because we had an incredible bond, we were wonderful at communication, and I really believe that we were already years beyond our expected maturity levels. Plus, my sister was a flight attendant, and I had the privilege of accessing her staff travel discounts, so I knew I could fly over to Adelaide for $33! So when, as some dumbass boys do, Jaryd made the decision to break up with me yet again – though not until he'd actually *arrived* in Adelaide (real nice, Cache) – it was time for me to put my big girl pants on. I knew he'd come back; he always did. I really did believe he loved me, but Jaryd was struggling with an internal battle between being so in love with someone he genuinely cared about at such a young age and living life as he wanted to as a nineteen-year-old boy. He wanted the freedom, he wanted to explore, he didn't want the pressures of being tied down in a committed relationship . . . but he loved me. So much.

So, what did I do? I offered him the chance to have both.

At 20 years of age, I recognised a bond that was powerful, yet one that was going to be challenged. Here was a boy, I realised, who was torn between love and life; and I understood that, at nineteen and 20 years old respectively, neither of us needed this pressure. Neither of us needed to be forcing a relationship that – purely down to logistics – would probably not work out, even though it was one that had a love and respect greater than anything I'd seen with other people my age. Yes, we were absolutely in love – but would a bit of freedom hurt anyone? Would it damage this connection?

I didn't think so, so I let him do what I believed he needed to do at that time. I let him go and 'scratch that itch', as they say. I gave him the freedom to be young, fun and single when he wasn't with me. But it wasn't all about him. I got the exact same freedom in return.

When we were together – if, say, by chance I got a weekend where I could fly over and visit him or he could pop back to Melbourne – we were 'together'. But when we were apart, we were free to do what we liked. It was a basic understanding that we both accepted, as it was fair, it was equal and, most importantly, it was honest. I would fly home from Adelaide, have a normal week at work and uni, then head out with my girlfriends on the weekend. There was never any expectation that we would speak on the phone every day, or that I needed to tell him where I was – and certainly not who I was with. And it went both ways. Not once did I ever ask him anything regarding his private business – if he'd slept with anyone else, who he was hooking up with, or what he was doing on a Saturday night. Still to this day, I have never asked him about that year. Why would I? What was it going to achieve? We had come to the agreement together, so finding out things like that would only risk hurt feelings. Why would we want to do that?

So, while many reports over the years claimed that Jaryd and I had an 'open relationship' the entire marriage, that is categorically incorrect. Yes, we were open at this stage, but we were so young and I knew it would benefit our relationship in the future. He needed to get some things out of his system and he deserved to do that. I didn't have the power to 'hold him down', nor would I ever want to do that to someone I loved. What right did I have over his life at nineteen? Forever is a really long time – and that's how long I believed this romance would last – so why not?

People really struggled to understand it, and a few of his alpha male (*cough highly insecure*) acquaintances tried more than once to intervene in our private business. Typical misogynistic males would lead the charge – the ones who would be quick to claim things like 'what happens on tour stays on tour', but were the first to question a female's actions, because 'how dare a woman be sexual or independent in her life choices!' In their eyes, I was a 'slut'. I was 'playing him' for living my own life back home – but, of course, Jaryd was a legend for pulling chicks every other weekend when I wasn't around. Over and over, Jaryd would tell them exactly where to go, but hey, fragile masculinity will always eventually catch up to those who stick to such outdated societal norms.

So many people couldn't wrap their heads around the idea that two mature young adults, at nineteen and 20, could communicate and navigate a sexually open and fluid relationship so well with each other. Or did it just make them uncomfortable, seeing two people going so far against what society had for so long deemed as 'normal'? Was me going against the grain – side by side with Jaryd, in a consensual, transparent and respectful agreement – going to mean I was ostracised yet again? So many people really didn't understand where we were coming from.

But they didn't *need* to understand, because it wasn't *for* them to understand.

When Jaryd returned to Melbourne the following year, we quickly got back together, and six months later, I was pregnant with our first baby, Bobby. We weren't trying, but we weren't *not* trying. I had underlying fertility issues that were diagnosed when I was seventeen – polycystic ovarian syndrome (PCOS) meant my ovaries were completely covered in cysts. Symptoms included acne, excessive body hair and an irregular menstruation cycle from my first period at fifteen. Jaryd and I loved the idea of having children together and very regularly discussed being young parents. So, when it happened unexpectedly on Father's Day 2013 – Jaryd just 21 at the time and me, 22 – it was met with much excitement.

Due to my ovarian issues, I actually hadn't had a period in more than eighteen months in the lead-up to my pregnancy, and I'd begun discussions with my mum about possibly freezing my eggs for use later in life. I started investigating natural ways to get my body 'working', as I would say, and discovered a Chinese acupuncturist in a shopping centre on my work break one day. 'PCOS HELP,' his sign said, and whilst I was totally naive to what this treatment might involve, I was willing to give anything a try, knowing that becoming a mum one day was something I desperately yearned for.

The man could not speak a word of English and I regret that I became frustrated when I couldn't communicate properly why I was there seeing him. My lack of ovulation over the years had left me tense and very sensitive around this issue, and in that moment, I began to cry knowing how much 'fixing' this meant to me. I took him out the front of his shop and I pointed to his sign.

'Baby?' he asked.

I nodded and he swiftly took me back into his room, laid me down on the table and started needling me across my lower abdomen and – weirdly, I thought at the time – my feet.

Always striving to approach life with an open mind, I took it for what it was: a few simple pricks, a hefty fee and a clip off my boss for returning ten minutes late to my shift.

My body had not bled in nearly two years, but within that month, she did. I'd never been so excited to see my blood-stained undies at the end of the day, and I told both Mum and Jaryd, filled with excitement over what it could mean.

Later next month, I popped out of the shower and walked past my mum, who was cooking dinner. (I was still living at home at this point.)

'Fucking hell, Mum, my nipples are so sore for some reason!' I told her. 'The water from the showerhead felt like razor blades on them!'

Without turning around, she let out a huff – a sound that sat somewhere between a scoff and an outright laugh – clearly finding humour in my naivety to the situation and well aware of what was happening to my body long before I had a clue.

You see, whilst the language barrier proved difficult for communication between me and that Chinese man, sitting in his shop window, his expertise allowed our souls to speak to one another. He changed my body that day; he changed my mind – and in doing so, he changed my entire life. I will forever be grateful to that man in his window.

Once my cycle began, I fell immediately pregnant with a little boy we referred to as our 'miracle baby'.

Chapter 6

I am a very sexual person, and I always have been. I've often joked that I must have gotten my sensuality from my mother. As young girls, my sisters and I would tease her about how much sex she and our dad must have had, because they had four kids.

'Only three times,' she'd joked in reply. 'Only had to do it once to get the twins.'

Sexuality has been a huge part of my life from a very young age. As I'm sure many children do, I would often explore my own anatomy and was very intrigued by what others' looked like. I don't ever recall getting a 'sex talk' from either of my parents – I think it was probably just assumed that, as the youngest of four girls, I'd figure it out myself somehow.

I do remember, however, being confused at a very young age as to why my vulva 'looked different' to my older sisters'. I would sit in the bath, staring downwards in fear and confusion – something I can't comprehend my now five-year-old daughter facing herself – and it led me down an extremely self-conscious path of sexual exploration in my early teens.

I have a vivid memory of being a little kid at my cousin's house, watching a movie, when a kissing scene came on. I had no idea what sex was at that stage, but as I watched that kissing scene, I felt a really hot and tingling sensation between my legs. I guess it would be the equivalent to a guy getting an erection for the first time, and I remember my confusion – but I also thought it felt really nice, not having any idea what was going on. So I knew what it was to be turned on from a young age – like, six or seven years old maybe? Looking back now, I was also regularly having orgasms in my sleep in my early teens, even though, again, I had no idea what was going on at the time. I would wake up from a dream to this amazing, pulsating feeling coursing through my body with no clue I'd just experienced an orgasm. This is something that still regularly occurs in my body, regardless of the amount of sex or masturbation I have or have not engaged in.

I can't speak for what goes on with sex education these days, but I strongly believe that sexual exploration wasn't talked about enough by adults when I was at school. It was all fear-mongering: 'Perform oral sex and you will contract herpes'; 'If you have sex you *will* get pregnant' (a completely false yet widely held assumption that many women often discover to be untrue only upon actually trying to conceive). At no point were sexual exploration or orientation discussed in so-called 'health' classes, and it certainly wasn't ever a conversation we had in my household. So, throughout my early teenage years, my friends and I would get our education the way so many young people do: by bouncing ideas off each other about what to do (and not do). There were also, of course, the widely held rules of schoolyard sex education. Prevalent themes were:

1. If you'd kissed a boy before reaching high school, you were epically cool.
2. If you hadn't had your first kiss by the end of Year Seven . . . hmm, awkward.
3. If you'd been fingered or touched a dick in Year Seven, you were a bit of a whore-bag – but if you hadn't done anything like that by the end of Year Eight . . . again, loser.

I fucking hate sitting here writing about myself from 20 years ago, but that was me, that was my friendship group – that was the 'norm' for teenagers in my area in the early 2000s. And weirdly enough, it was the norm for everyone to be clued-in to what other people were doing, too. You knew when someone from another school had been fingered at the formal afterparty. You knew who'd disappeared down to the back paddock and dropped to their knees at so-and-so's sixteenth birthday party. And you *definitely* knew if anyone had sex – because, 'Woah, can you believe they actually did it?!'

As I developed, I continued to be extremely self-conscious about my body. I always had *huge* boobs, a lot bigger than my friends', and whilst theirs all sat nice, at that age, mine did not – and I hated them. Being much bigger than your average fifteen-year-old, I hated the way they looked, I hated the way they felt . . . I just *despised* them. For this reason, the early days of my own sexual exploration consisted of a lot of giving. I wasn't confident enough to let my walls down, to expose my own body, so I would allow my sensuality to ooze out by way of my passion for giving other people pleasure. My jaw clenches at the thought of it now, but I loved the position of power that performing oral sex on a male gave me. It was always my favourite thing to do.

I used to think I liked it because I knew that I was good at it, but as I've grown up, I've realised it was being in a position of power that I loved. It made me feel great to pleasure somebody. It gave me this sense of power. I savoured those moments when a guy always thought he was in control, and I loved letting them *believe* that – letting them think that they were calling the shots, that I was only between their thighs because they wanted me there, because I was a slave to their domination, their masculinity. But what they didn't know, what no man ever realised, was that no-one ever got me between their legs (or found themselves between mine) unless I chose it. I was the one who made the decision to be there – not them.

When Kendall Jenner and Phoenix Suns basketball star Devin Booker's relationship made headlines in 2020, after the reality star had publicly dated a string of NBA players, trolls on Twitter commented that the boys must be passing her around. Her mic-drop-moment reply was me through and through: 'They act like I ain't in charge of where I throw this cooch.' Fifteen-year-old Sophie had that exact mentality, and 31-year-old Sophie most certainly still does now.

Though I am thrilled with the generation coming through being open to empowering individuals for traits that were once deemed taboo, the patriarchy *does* still exist. When I was younger, girls who openly enjoyed being sexual – whether they'd had two partners or 20 – were instantly branded 'sluts' or 'whores' by their male peers. It's a horrifically outdated view and one I can only describe as foul – a view neither my son nor daughter will ever be exposed to under my roof. I see myself as a real-life future Jean Milburn – the outspoken and well-known sex therapist character in the hit Netflix series *Sex Education* – providing my children with extensive knowledge of both sex and relationship psychology.

But, whilst I was always very sexual, I actually didn't have a huge number of partners in my teenage years and early twenties, because I was always in serious long-term relationships. At fifteen, I was having sex with a friend who wasn't officially my boyfriend, however we slept together regularly and exclusively for the majority of the year. Then in Year Eleven, I was in a relationship with another boy for nearly two years. I was with someone who I can see was a total fuck-stain after that. (I like to think of that as my greatest insult – I actually imagine a flaky, smelly, crusty stain on the carpet left over from some bad sex.) And then I met Jaryd at 20 years old and ended up marrying him.

Jaryd and I had always shared the same views on sex. Ever since we first got together, we have both always believed that humans aren't meant to only be with one person sexually. In our personal view, it is a fairy tale to believe that one person can forever meet *all* of our emotional and sexual needs. I'm not denying that such love and commitment can exist for others – and I'm never one to judge another's choice. This was merely our view and one we couldn't see longevity without. We'd had many conversations from the early days in our relationship, and had always agreed that we didn't believe sexual monogamy was natural for mammals.

For me, relationships need to have mutual consent, respect, flexibility, empathy, communication, care and adaptability. And whilst monogamy is the dominant pattern amongst western society, I know many people in relationships who preach monogamy, yet lack basic skills like open communication, honesty and respect. And whilst society has conditioned us to believe that monogamy is the ethical and moral choice, infidelities often seem to be the cause for relationship breakdowns and divorce.

Is monogamy the right thing to do when, in so many relationships, there are inconsistent standards between what one person believes they can do and what they expect of their partner?

When a friend from school who married her childhood sweetheart – a woman who has never had a sexual experience with another human, who is now pregnant with her second child, who classifies herself as monogamous – proclaims after sinking one too many glasses of rosé with the girls that she has 'settled' in life and lives in fear she will get 'bored'?

Whilst many would think that an open sexual relationship is detrimental to your commitment, Jaryd and I were always of the belief that this choice actually highlighted our deep love for each other. Our communication, trust, honesty and respect for each other's needs far outweighed an outdated interpretation of what a 'successful, happy relationship' looked like. Besides, each of us allowing the other to be pleasured provided us with great pleasure in return.

It was more than love for us, too. It was the common ground we shared for our sensuality and sexual desires in life – something Jaryd always allowed me to express without judgement. We both always wanted to try new things and respected each other enough to not be intimidated by what the other person wanted or needed in their life.

A lot of people heard that we were 'swingers' – but I can assure you that's far from the truth. Trust me, we tried our best to find adult parties that catered and suited to us both but never had any luck! We did share a partner-swapping experience with someone from Jaryd's circle and his wife one night – something that had been built up over a few months in a playful group chat – but in our view, it was very underwhelming.

One year, I hired Jaryd two escorts for his birthday present, as living out a two-to-one threesome was a fantasy of his. Despite the girls asking me, I didn't partake because I wanted that to be purely Jaryd's experience – it was his birthday, after all, and it was his moment to enjoy.

But let's pretend we were swingers. Let's pretend we engaged in fetish play or frequently hired professional sex workers to partake in activities with us. Why, as two consenting adults, is this in any way an issue for anyone else? It wasn't something we openly spoke about – believe it or not, we *did* actually maintain some privacy during our time together – but it's also not something we are ashamed of, nor should we be.

While sex can be interpreted differently by every individual, to us, it was one of the most natural things we did.

~

While I was always very open sexually and I have always owned my sensual nature, I've often been made to feel that, as a woman, there's something wrong with me. Whenever I'd speak to some girlfriends about sex as an adult, wanting to ask them questions or spilling about an experience like you would want to with your friends, they'd roll their eyes.

'Oh Sophie . . . you're disgusting.'

'You are out of control.'

'What on earth is wrong with you?'

(It appears that whilst owning my sexuality, I wasn't facing up to the fact I might not have been hanging out with like-minded people . . .)

Ever since I was sixteen, I've been able to have casual sex without getting tangled up in emotions, and many guys over the years have called me a unicorn because of it. 'You're not fucking real,' they've said, unable to believe that a woman can just enjoy sex for what it is and not get emotionally attached. I know the many stereotypes that have existed surrounding women and attachment, however the older I've gotten and the more I've aligned myself with people who have similar values to mine, the more I've come to realise that it actually isn't uncommon for females to be able to separate sex from emotion – not quite on par with the assumptions made of us. Intensities of both desire and arousal vary vastly between people, and there are strong messages of acceptance around women who have little to no libido. But I have always pushed to validate the feelings of those women who, like myself, crave pleasure and variety, and those who seek to continually evolve for the purpose of sexual adventure by living out real-life fantasies.

As recently as a couple of years ago, while I was between partners, I was sleeping with a female friend of mine. We had both separated from our girlfriends, we both got what we wanted, and we're still really good friends to this day.

In 2020, in between a horrific breakup and getting back with my current partner, I was, once again, seeking pleasure. I've found sex with females for me to be more intimate, more emotional – wild and dirty at times, yes, but also more spiritual. But what I needed that night was for someone to really throw me around. I needed to be absolutely dominated, to be fucked. So I invited a male friend of mine over, we hung out and we watched a basketball game, and as it was getting quite late, I asked him outright, 'Okay, are we going to have sex?' I told him to give me five minutes while I changed my sheets for him and then it was literally like an exchange of service. He bent me over on the bed and I soon ended up with my head banging on my bed head – it was one of those nights, and I had certainly wasted my time putting clean sheets on. There was no emotion involved, just a mutual, consensual understanding that we were providing satisfaction for each other. We high-fived on the way out and we're still mates to this day.

Chapter 7

My open views on sex and sexuality were often a point of contention (though hardly the only one) between myself and my high-school acquaintances, and they contributed to my being the 'odd one out' well into my mid-twenties. We'd go out for big group dinners, all of us and our partners, but Jaryd would always know to save me a seat down the boys' end of the table. I would sit on the border between the sexes, with the girls on one side of me and the guys on the other. Since having my children young, I became less and less interested in their conversations. What they spoke about didn't always fulfil me, it didn't enlighten me, nor inspire any new ways of thinking. It was all who's-earning-what at their jobs, which random girl we weren't even friends with anymore had put on weight, and 'OMG did you see who she's dating?' That just wasn't me. It wasn't personal – it was just that, after entering motherhood, a lot of conversations about other people did not interest me.

I've also always maintained incredible friendships with guys, whereas I've always struggled with the female relationships that exist within large female-led groups. I never liked the 'hierarchy' system that operated, where one or two girls 'led' all the decision-making while the conforming group members below followed suit. I did find that some of the girls I used to know were more inclined to follow crowds and form cliques – and YUCK. Gross. Nope. The second I see cliquiness start, I'm out, because if I can't be free to be who I am in an open, accepting environment, I'm much happier on my own – staying in my own lane, choosing my own direction. In that sense, I've always been passionate about never following the crowd and I hope that by living life as I do so openly on socials and in this book, I can inspire women everywhere to do the same. I touched on it before but being intimidated by someone's confidence or threatened by their own self-pride does not give you the right to judge their character – it only highlights your own fear of what you'll find if you do a little self-reflection.

Until very recently, I was never brave enough to really trust my intuition around this topic (though experience later taught me how crucial she is). Every year, we would all get together for a big girls' lunch, and it really was so much fun. We'd obviously see each other on and off during the year, but it was great to have a big annual catch up with everyone and reflect on the year that was. I do think long-term female friendships are important, and I maintain now that some of my best girlfriends are the ones I've known for ten to fifteen years. And whilst I find the older you get, the busier you get and the less time you have for regular catch-ups, the peace found in those long-standing relationships during difficult circumstances is just beautiful.

But for the past couple of years, I would get a lot of anxiety in the lead-up to the 'Girls' Lunch' simply because I didn't feel like I fitted in with my friends anymore. Not that I ever really did, but as I got older it was becoming more and more obvious to me just how 'other' I felt around them. My intuition was telling me, 'These aren't your people; you don't belong.'

'I want to go see them, but I just can't be fucked,' I remember telling Jaryd one year. I didn't feel like I had the right energy to bring to the day, and I wouldn't be able to enjoy myself. Their concerns – while so normal, so typical of single twenty-somethings at that stage of life – were no longer ones I shared.

I wanted to talk about something that mattered to me – how their mental health was going, whether or not they were happy in life, or what they were looking forward to most – not, say, the size of someone's engagement ring, which is the kind of topic that would often come up.

'Perhaps it's all the couple in question could afford,' I would think. Maybe the bride-to-be didn't even *want* a big diamond. Or maybe, just maybe, it has nothing to do with us? Where's it written in the book of life that you have to have a big engagement ring? How does that make you a better person? To many of my acquaintances, a ring was a status symbol but for me, all that mattered was that the person in question was happy . . . and all I could think about was when the hell lunch would be served so I could get home and sing *Twinkle Twinkle Little Star* to my babies.

Don't get me wrong, I have expensive tastes for myself. I know that, and I am proud of the fact that I will treat myself and others around me, but I certainly don't have any expectations for others. I've never done anything to impress other people – an external opinion has no impact on my actions. Too many people are still caught up in the image and perception they believe they must maintain, that they need to seek happiness and approval from people who have no role to play in how their own lives plays out. My theory has always been, if it *has* nothing to do with me, then it *is* nothing to do with me.

When Jaryd and I got engaged, for example, he gave me a black diamond ring. Now, black diamonds are absolutely beautiful, they're very unique, and they're not cheap, but they're typically not as expensive as white diamonds. But I didn't need that. I didn't need the size, the carats, the price point as a symbol of Jaryd's love for and commitment to me. If anything, I wanted Jaryd to design a unique piece for me in his taste and a style that truly represented us − and that's exactly what he did. It was a thick platinum band with 60 mini diamonds and a two-and-a-half carat black diamond in the middle.

Upon seeing it, I knew I never wanted two rings, either; I didn't want the traditional engagement ring and separate wedding ring. My 80-year-old nan was shocked. 'But no one will know you're married!'

If I was going to have piece of jewellery on my finger for the rest of my life, I wanted it to be exactly what I wanted, and not something that − again − society had told me I'm supposed to have. So, I was more than happy with that ring as both my 'engagement' and 'wedding' ring. It was simply perfect as it was.

One of my friends later told me an acquaintance had been talking about it behind my back.

'A black diamond? What, because they can't afford a real one?'

And sure, it was rude, but more than anything I couldn't figure out why anyone would care enough to speak about it. Why did my ring have to have a white diamond? How did it impact their life if we could or couldn't afford a 'real' diamond? Why was something that should be enthusiastically celebrated a competition?

It was hurtful. It really did weigh me down for a long time, moments like this, from people who I knew – and who knew me. Why did some feel the need to criticise my fiancé's personal choice? He had gone and created something that he liked, a piece I would treasure forever and give to my kids someday.

I saw a similar theme when it came to choosing my wedding dress. Completely bucking archaic traditions, I didn't wear white. There were many reasons, one of them being that white as a wedding dress colour has historically been linked to the idea of purity, innocence and virginity – and whilst I wasn't completely against a white dress, that particular notion didn't align with me. But it was actually Jaryd who finally persuaded me.

'It's not that I can't find nice dresses. I can,' I told him. 'I just don't know if a white wedding dress is for me.'

He'd always loved me in black – in very classic, Audrey Hepburn style – and he knew how much I loved wearing black. So when he said, so simply, 'Why don't you wear black?', that was it. That was as much thought as I put into it. I had a gorgeous dress made, I felt like a million dollars, Jaryd was just beaming at the end of the aisle . . . And yet so many people thought I was doing it to get attention. If they only knew the conversation we'd had, the struggle I was having to find a wedding dress that I loved, and how one little suggestion by my gorgeous man had made so much sense!

It wasn't a calculated move to get social media attention or grab news headlines. It was just me doing *exactly* what I wanted to do.

~

A number of my people in my old social networks were into party drugs when we were younger, too – and, again, I'm not expressing this from a place of judgement. I honestly couldn't care less, and even now, I know a lot of people in their late twenties and thirties who experiment with recreational drugs. I tried drugs when I was around eighteen – ecstasy on two occasions, cocaine once, speed once – but it never really did anything for me, and my anxiety around the thought of my body being 'out of my control' was rife, so I tried and then opted out all within the one year. Another decision made on my own, one that would only ever impact me, that was again judged by others. Some people seemed to think that I made these decisions because I believed I was better than them. This was far from the truth, as I regularly enjoyed a cigarette, despite knowing how unhealthy that was for me. The humour I found in being 'jokingly' called disgusting for smoking by 'classy' individuals, who would snort perfectly straight cocaine lines off filthy surfaces in toilet cubicles . . . I do think drugs as a whole are gross and the social acceptance around them these days is incredibly unsafe, but it's none of my business what people do to their own bodies.

But as usual, I was the black sheep, the odd one out, and I was excluded for my choices.

I guess, looking at it now, I could have definitely been giving off the vibe that I was being judgmental. I cannot stress enough that it was nothing to do with the drug use itself. It was more around the divide that drugs can cause between people. I didn't enjoy myself anymore around those acquaintances who were taking drugs and it caused me a lot of anxiety whenever I was in a situation where others were doing it because I *knew* I wouldn't enjoy myself, and I needed to accept that for what it was.

Recognising that certain people or situations no longer serve you can be very difficult. It can be hard to let go. But life has taught me that holding on longer than you need to, becomes taxing on you emotionally, spiritually and physically, and I was too focused on being the best mother I could be, as well as getting the very best out of myself, to hold on any longer.

Chapter 8

I am and always have been a very confident person. If ever I do a public speaking gig, or an open Q&A with my followers, I'm often asked how I became to be so naturally self-assured, but the truth is, I don't really know for sure.

I have vivid memories of always being the 'loud' one in the family; the typical little sister, gloating and show-ponying her way through the house so everyone could see her. I was different at school, though – never the class clown, reserved, embarrassed to stand in front of a crowd, similar to what I see in my own son now.

'Presence', as I will call it, is something I have had though my entire life. Perhaps because I was always so much taller than my peers (I was the tallest person in Year Six, out of both the boys and the girls – just before the boys' balls dropped and their heights skyrocketed). It's true that I have been this way my entire life, and whilst I have had to fine-tune my own mindset at times, I was born with the idea that no one can nor should tell me who I want to be. Part of this I put down to being the youngest of four girls in a household where I had to learn very early on to back myself. Whilst I think my eldest sister's confidence was slightly dismantled after the arrival of twin sisters, leading her to require a deeper sense of acceptance and assurance from people as she's gotten older, I went the other way, knowing I had to do most of it myself because no one else was going to do it for me.

Society has regularly shown us – or even *taught* us – that whilst men are allowed to proudly overestimate their strengths and abilities, women are to do the total opposite.

I have often been referred to as 'arrogant' – 'Ugh, you love yourself so much!' I've had people say that to me – and it's something we see a hell of a lot within prominent media platforms in today's society. Any sign of a woman displaying self-love, whether for her talents, her looks or her abilities, is deemed vain and egotistical.

To me, arrogance comes into play in social hierarchies. It's an attitude that says, 'I am better than you and I don't even need to waste my time explaining why.' It's rudeness, an exaggerated sense of self-importance and entitlement, and looking down on those they deem inferior, never entertaining the idea of a friendship or a conversation with those they feel 'don't matter'.

Confidence, on the other hand, I believe stems from true self-worth. Someone willing to both take – and show – pride in their achievements and failures, without having ego interfere. Confident people, whilst self-assured, are good listeners, too, willing to take on feedback for the sake of self-improvement. And lastly, people with confidence are not scared – not scared to make mistakes, not scared to take risks, and not scared to shine a light on others doing well, either.

The lines between confidence and arrogance have far too long been blurred and it's so refreshing to see the youth of today changing that language and narrative.

One of my favourite Instagram pages to follow is that of Chantelle Otten. As both an author and sexologist from Australia, Chantelle has educated me so much on the acceptance of my sexual nature as a woman, and to be extremely proud of it. An empowering woman, advocating for discussions that were (and, in many areas, still are) considered highly taboo, Chantelle leads the way to champion all humans' self-esteem, individuality and our right to express ourselves in any way we wish.

More and more, we are seeing women take ownership of their lives, their bodies, their own worth – without the need for validation or approval. We are becoming more accepting of each other, warts 'n' all, and speaking positively about ourselves is beginning to be praised.

I don't apologise for my confidence, because it's who I am – and in a world where we're forever being told to 'love yourself', I have found it difficult at times when I've come under criticism for doing exactly that. A confident Sophie is not me sitting here, telling you that I am perfect, that I've never made mistakes in life, or done things that I regret. That would be far from the truth. But a confident Sophie *does* sit here and admit all those things, whilst accepting them, taking ownership for my faults, proudly knowing that I have reflected and learnt from them. That you, in fact, do not need to be 'good' at something in order to be a confident person. A confident person accepts themselves for who they are, regardless of external opinions.

My personality – my inherent 'me-ness' – does make some people uncomfortable, which is completely unintentional on my part, and I have struggled with that. But I also think, in a way, it's helped me be successful and confident online. People have made assumptions about me my whole life, and I've just had to learn not to care; to become completely immune to the outside noise. When someone has formed a perception of you, even if it's incorrect, their mind is usually made up – you'll rarely have the ability to change that, particularly when you're dealing with, say, online trolls, nor should you *ever* put that pressure on yourself to do so. A person who has made a judgement on your character without direct communication with you or being in an informed position *cannot* be valued by you. I always say that in order to value someone's opinion of me, I have to first respect that person. And I will never respect people who believe that critiquing others' life choices from afar is an honourable act.

It's also so deeply engrained in women to back away from praise, to shoot down compliments, that when someone owns and accepts herself, it can come as shock to other people! But I refuse to make myself small for society. If someone says, 'I love your dress', I don't say, 'Oh, it's really old', or, 'OMG I look so fat in this.' I say, 'Thank you.' Or, 'Isn't the colour beautiful?' And I say it every bloody time because, frankly, if I'm wearing it, I feel good in it, and I'm not going to dismiss someone who goes out of their way to compliment me. Of course, you've got to have a bit of modesty somewhere in there, too! But I will always thank someone who has gone to the effort of telling me that I look great, and that surprises a lot of people because it's so unheard of for a woman to own herself in that way.

Loving myself just as much in PJs on the couch, no makeup, bags under the eyes, greasy hair thrown into a messy bun has also been crucial to my mindset – we're equally worthy no matter what we're looking like. Yet this has not been the message society has always sent us.

Even my four-year-old daughter is already telling me she's not beautiful unless she's dressed up in a pink, frilly, fairy dress. Somewhere along the way, Florence has been conditioned to believe that she's only 'pretty' when she's in a pink dress, that she's only beautiful when she's carrying a little handbag, wearing lipstick. Now, I've raised both my kids in the exact same way, never gender specific and have allowed them to make their own choices and develop their own interests. Somehow, though, Floss is still very stereotypically 'girly'. She loves her dolls, her favourite colour is pink, and she regularly uses phrases such as 'boys can't wear that' (referring to dresses and skirts), despite our household never using language like that. Once she was wearing a T-shirt and leggings when I hugged her, gave her a cuddle and told her she's beautiful.

She said, 'No, Mummy! Look at me! I'm not pretty now!'

Oh my God. What the fuck have I done wrong?

But I know this didn't come from me. From any of the parents and role models around her. It's society. This has come from TV, or YouTube, or maybe at kinder. And it further cements the fact that we all need to stop, as a society, only telling girls they're beautiful when they're dressed a certain way. Stop telling little girls they're pretty when they've got their hair brushed nicely, when they put on their mummy's lipstick, and start telling them they're beautiful all the damn time. That beauty isn't just aligned with physical appearance. We need to highlight the importance of a beautiful personality, a beautiful nature, a beautiful outlook on life.

There is something very fucking wrong with society when a four-year-old has been conditioned to believe she's only pretty when she's wearing her princess dress.

Chapter 9

As confident as I've always been, my self-assuredness did get a little shake-up when I was faced with the realisation that I was attracted to women.

Well, *a* woman.

At that stage, when I met *her* at the panel in 2017, she was still the only female I'd found myself attracted to.

I was still as certain of myself in all other facets of my life but finding myself crushing on a girl did throw me out. I didn't know what was going on, I didn't understand my feelings – but a few months after we'd met, my desire to get to know her better hadn't faded at all. She and I were in touch here and there on social media, but that was as far as it went. Nothing had changed. You probably wouldn't even call us 'friends' – we were in that weird space between, where you're more than acquaintances, but not quite close enough to call each other mates. We'd chat when I'd go to her footy games with Jaryd and the kids (as Jaryd became quite friendly with her, too). He is obviously a massive advocate for women's sport and he used to play football for Carlton, so they'd hang out a bit and she'd bounce ideas off him, that sort of thing.

One night in early November, I was flicking through Instagram, having a casual stalk, when I realised something was missing. Her girlfriend wasn't in any of her recent photos. In fact . . . *scrolling back, scrolling back* . . . she hadn't been in any posts for a while.

Has she broken up with her girlfriend? Does this mean she's single?

I shouldn't have cared.

I shouldn't have.

But I did. God, I cared. So, so much.

The thought that she might be out of a relationship excited me. *What the fuck?* There I was, married, but getting such a kick out of the idea that my pretend girlfriend (as she'd become in my mind) – who doesn't *know* she's my pretend girlfriend – had broken up with her *actual* girlfriend . . .

I became obsessed with finding out whether they'd split, so I started poking around to find out if she was officially on the market, if this fantasy I'd dreamed up in my head was real. I tiptoed around it, chatting to her on Instagram and asking how things were going – as if I hadn't already guessed.

'Oh no, we actually broke up a few months ago,' she told me.

'Oooh, I'm so sorry.'

I feigned shock and sadness.

'If you ever need anyone to talk to or want to bounce things off me . . .'

Ugh. I was getting way too much pleasure out of her being single. It sounds just so fucked to admit that out loud, but it's the truth – and again, it wasn't something I was hiding from my husband. I told Jaryd as soon as I found out they'd broken up!

'Well you're in now, go on then!' he joked.

Was I in? No . . . there's no way.

So, when she messaged me out of the blue asking if she could come to my office one morning, I was shocked.

'Hey, are you at work today? I've got something for you.'

Oh my God.

'Yeah sure, the address is . . .'

What could she possibly have for me?

She arrived at my office in Port Melbourne, we hugged and chatted for a while, friendly as usual. Then she reached into her bag and pulled out a tiny footy jumper for my baby, Florence. Up until that point, I'd been convinced I was caught up in my own little fantasy – nothing more than a dumb little crush. It didn't occur to me for a second that this incredible, strong, sexy woman could possibly be sharing the same feelings for me.

Is she just doing this to be nice, to be a good friend?

Does she buy all of her friends jumpers for their kids?

But we don't even really know each other.

Why is she doing this?

Is this normal . . .?

She'd driven into my office specially, she'd bought my daughter a gift . . . Even though I was starting to wonder if there was something more on her side, I still assumed she only wanted to be friends with me. But looking back now, I can see that there must have been something about me that intrigued her, too. Because really, who was I to her? I was nobody – just some chick she'd met at a speaking event. We'd been friends on Instagram, we'd run into each other a bit here and there, said 'hi' at a footy game or two . . . but there was no long-standing friendship there. She certainly didn't have to buy footy jumpers for my kids. But whether either of us liked to admit it, there was a connection there. Whether that was a friendship or more, well . . . that was yet to unfold.

I thanked her for the gift, we grabbed some lunch and sat talking for almost two hours – about footy, about her breakup, about what was coming up for her career . . . we had a really great chat, and for the first time since I met her, I felt like I could relax. I wasn't nervous anymore. I did feel like a genuine, beautiful friendship could form now. She was no longer some hot girl I messaged on Instagram; she was a really interesting person and I wanted to get to know her better. My intense (in hindsight, slightly creepy) obsession began to cool off, transforming into a genuine friendship with this woman who, months earlier, had set my soul on fire with one glance.

The better I got to know her, the closer friends we became. We were texting, calling, hanging out and I wasn't some giddy schoolgirl with a crush anymore. When we'd met, I think my obsession was fuelled by the fact that I didn't know her. She had been so mysterious; this woman who was somehow also masculine, who made my stomach do backflips with her piercing eyes. Now, a full year on from that crazy first meeting, I still thought she was attractive – and there was something simmering away underneath the surface – but Jaryd and I were in a really good place at this point, and I had gotten pretty good at ignoring that niggling feeling that I wanted something more than friendship with this woman.

At this stage, Jaryd and I had already begun to discuss options regarding our relationship moving forward (totally separate from this woman), weighing up if either of us wanted to actually be married anymore. Neither of us had ever really wanted to follow traditional norms, and we'd openly discussed our annoyance with ourselves for rushing so quickly to do something we thought we 'had to' do. But my logical brain rushed into play, insisting I needed to make giving our relationship another crack my utmost priority.

That was until the three of us went out for lunch one day.

Jaryd and I were heading to a café and I flicked her a text asking her to join us. We were all mates – why not ask her to come along? The conversation turned to sex, as it often does with adult friends, and when Jaryd got up to go to the bathroom, I found myself asking her about how women have sex with other women.

'How do girls have sex?' I asked, point blank.

'What do you mean?!' she laughed.

'Like . . . is it hands? Is it tongues? What counts as sex?'

I was so naive.

She grabbed my hand from across the table, looked into my eyes and tapped on my long pink acrylic nails.

'Well, for starters, you're going to have to get rid of those.'

I. Fucking. Died. The way she touched me, the way those eyes shot straight to my soul . . . If I were a guy – if I could have an erection in that moment – the whole table would have moved. Just like that, I was in love with her again.

Is she being cheeky? Can she tell that I'm into her?

Oh my God, I've got to get rid of my nails. That's it, I'm cutting my nails off.

There's this joke within the gay community – it's very stereotypical, but it's just a joke, really – that you can tell if a girl's gay if she's got short nails. And looking back now, it's funny because that was one of the first things I noticed about her – I couldn't fathom why her nails were cut so brutally short. I also realised later that I started doing little things like

96

that, like cutting my nails. I still wasn't consciously contemplating sleeping with a girl . . . but did some part of me want to maybe start putting out a vibe that I wanted to? Yes. Absolutely. I wanted to cut my nails short so that this woman might think that I'm a lesbian. It was so out of character for me to do anything to create an impression, but something was happening to me.

Meanwhile, Jaryd had given me the green light to explore this fantasy.

'Go for it,' he'd said.

Jaryd's like me, he can separate sex from emotion, and we both got really turned on watching each other kiss other people. I loved seeing him pursue another girl at a nightclub and kiss her, and it was the same for him. It was just our thing, we liked it. Every human and every relationship, regardless of the dynamic, is entitled to have their own way of doing things, especially when it comes to their own fantasies. We were just so turned on by each other, even if that meant being with other people.

So that's why, when this arose, he so enthusiastically urged me to explore it. That was just us. I know a lot of people would think, 'I can't believe that he let her do that,' or 'I can't believe she did that while she was married,' but that was just the way we worked. Again, society tells us we're not supposed to be okay with talking about things like that, you know? You're not supposed to tell people that stuff.

So, just like that, my crush-turned-friend was now my reignited obsession . . . and my hall pass.

'I'm not just going to go up to her and say, "Hey, do you want to have sex with me? I'm married. And I've never done it with a girl before. But, like, do you want to do it?"' I laughed to Jaryd as we spoke about it for about the millionth time.

'And what if I don't like a vagina? And like . . . how do you do it? What do I do to it?'

'Well, you've got one . . .' he trailed off.

'Yeah, but I don't do all of those things myself!'

Truth be told, I didn't even know if I *wanted* to have sex with her. I did want to kiss her, though – that much I knew. I'd never wanted to kiss a girl in my life, but I was so fucking sexually attracted to this woman, I was obsessed with the idea of exploring that with her . . .

Jaryd and I would talk about it, plan out the scenario together, discuss how I was going to do it. My husband, who I was still very much in love with, was like my bro, my wingman, talking me through it.

I began to step things up. I flirted more. I dropped hints. I wanted her to know what my intentions were, but I didn't want her to think I was doing anything wrong by Jaryd – and that is a tricky thing to convey to someone when you operate in such an open dynamic. It can be confronting to those who don't have the same moral views, and I completely respect that. She could well have assumed I was trying to have an affair behind my husband's back. And it's not like you can just DM someone on Instagram saying, 'Hey, I want to explore this with you, don't worry my husband said it's fine.' What if she thought I was some kind of freak? Or I'd totally misread the whole situation and she actually only thought of me as a friend?

But I also knew what I wanted – and when I know what I want, I get it.

And I knew, I *knew*, she was interested in me too, in some way or another – even if she wasn't on the same level as me. I had to put it out there – so I did one day, during one of our Instagram chats.

'So, how's single life?' I asked.

'Yeah, good, you know.'

Time to do this.

'You know, I think I'd be jealous if you had a new girl-friend . . .'

It was on the table, finally, but she didn't pick up the hint – or if she did, she didn't do anything with it. Actually, she kind of ignored me until I prodded again – at which point she put me straight into the friend zone. I'd allowed myself to be extremely vulnerable at this point, risking this friendship we'd built, but I was also aware of exactly how forthright it may have sounded.

'I think we're just friends, Soph.'

Damn.

But I had a feeling she only said that because I was married and, as far as she was concerned, that made me off limits. I needed her to know that it was fine with Jaryd.

'Of course,' I replied. 'But I think you're smart enough to know what I'm thinking.'

'Yeah,' she replied. '. . . I've always known what you're thinking.'

So she admitted it. She knew – she'd always known – that I'd been into her.

~

A couple of weeks later, I was out for dinner and drinks with some friends. One girlfriend and I had had a couple more cocktails than everyone else and when they were getting ready to go home, we decided we wanted to go out. I hadn't gone out in forever and it was completely random that I was struck by the sudden urge to go dancing, but my friend Amelia was single and always up for a good time so off we went. We headed to some bar in Toorak with another mate, but it was terrible, so we admitted defeat, jumped in the car and headed home not long after.

As we wove our way through Melbourne's busy lit-up streets, I jumped on Instagram for a scroll.

Wait, she's out tonight, too?

There it was, on her stories. My crush was in the city. It was unheard of – she rarely drank, hardly ever went out . . . She was every bit the professional athlete, and even though it was off season, I was shocked to see her in a bar with mates on a night out.

Things had gotten a bit weird after our last conversation and we hadn't spoken in a while. I felt like I'd completely embarrassed myself and lost my chance at even a friendship with her, so I had stepped back and given both of us the space that we needed.

But the night was young and the cocktails I'd thrown back at dinner had made me bold.

'Oi, where are ya?'

Is she even going to reply?

. . .

'In Richmond, where are you?'

Oh my God she wrote back. Straightaway.

Shit, where are we?

I opened Google Maps, searched for the club she'd mentioned. We were right around the corner, two minutes away, actually.

'Stop the car!' I shrieked.

I turned to my friend, beside me in the backseat. She knew about my little crush.

'You've got to take one for the team and come out with me.'

Indecision played on her face.

'C'mon! We wanted to go out, where we went was just shit but this is going to be fun, I promise. She's with a whole group of girls . . .'

'But I don't know anyone,' she countered.

'Neither do I!'

I knew *her* though. And I was looking great. I'd had a few cocktails ... and we'd spoken numerous times in the past about how fun a night out together would be. Of course, I'd envisaged kissing her, and I knew that it would only happen if we were having a drunk night out together. I wouldn't have been brave enough to make a move without a few drinks in my system, and I was aware she wasn't the type to do so, either.

I looked at my friend, begging silently.

'All right, I'll come.'

It felt like it was meant to be. Everything had worked in my favour that night – we happened to be out, we wanted to go out dancing, *she* was out that night, my friend agreed to come with me ... If she'd said no, there's no way I'd have gone alone. This couldn't be a coincidence, some chance encounter. This was alignment.

Yet as excited as I was, with butterflies in my stomach, I was also still trying to understand why I felt this way about a girl.

I'm straight.

I am married.

I shouldn't be attracted to her.

But I am.

I walked up the stairs to the Richmond Club, nerves gripping my stomach a little tighter with every step I took.

It was thrilling. And scary. And incredible. I was bouncing with excitement as I strode through the door, heading straight for the bar to grab a drink. I didn't want to look like I was looking for her, like I was trying to find someone in the crowd. I wanted to look self-assured, certain . . .

Ding! My phone buzzed in my hand.

'Where are you?'

It was *her*.

'We're at the bar.'

Two seconds later, there she was, hitting me like a ton of bricks all over again. Hair up in a bun, no makeup, plain black T-shirt and jeans combo, cool Asics runners . . . *Why am I attracted to that?*

She didn't look the way I would've ever expected someone I'd find attractive to look. But then there was her − 10 out of 10. Fucking perfection.

She grabbed my hand and my heart leapt into my throat as I tried not to overthink the move. After all, you grab your friends' hands in night clubs, too, right? It doesn't necessarily mean anything. But I liked it; I liked that I was walking through a nightclub with this girl holding my hand. It felt . . . right. She led me over to her group of friends, introduced me to everyone, shouting over the pumping bass coming from the nearby speaker. They were all dressed the same way as her − tees, sneakers, jeans. Fuck, they looked comfortable. I knew I looked good when I left the house earlier that night, but I suddenly wished I was wearing something other than my leather pants, my giant hoop earrings, my silver 12cm-high heeled boots.

'What the fuck are you wearing those shoes for?' one of the girls shouted, laughing over the music.

Not a bad question. Seeing these girls out in T-shirts and jeans – I fucking wanted to wear that out. Sure, I guess I always could have, but I didn't grow up with the belief that it was okay to wear that for a night out. I grew up in a world where you wore high heels when you went out, you wore false lashes and you had your lipstick on and you had your hair done, because that's what 'girls' wear. And then here's this group of chicks, beers in hand, having the best time on the dance floor, not giving a fuck what anyone else thought . . . There was no going to the bathroom in a horde, no bitching about what someone else was wearing, no fighting or drama. The simplicity promised in a night out with this group of women was instantly appealing. It was just a group of girls out having fun.

I didn't realise it at the time, but in that moment, I began to find my place.

~

We were openly flirty all night. None of her friends knew who I was, but it was pretty damn obvious that there was some chemistry between us. She introduced me as her friend, but it didn't take long before her friends started asking me what was going on with us.

'Oh no, nothing.' I laughed.

They could tell I was lying. One minute, their mate had disappeared into the crowd and the next, she'd come back holding hands with this tall, brunette girly-girl. Amongst a bunch of fellow gay women, it was probably a fair assumption to make.

'Bullshit, look at you two! You're all over each other.'

And we were.

I could tell she was having fun. She was certainly pushing the boundaries and I think she was enjoying the attention of it all. I knew what her intentions were when we went up to the bar. Upon me asking her what she wanted to drink, she told me she was driving, but in seeing the slight disappointment on my face, she asked if I wanted her to have a few drinks with me. I gave her a little smile and she ordered herself a wet pussy shot followed immediately by a vodka and soda, her hand around my back the whole time.

We were acting like a couple. Everywhere we went we were holding hands. We were close on the dance floor. All of her friends were convinced we'd been sleeping together and it was very clear to me that, oh my fucking God, I am going to kiss her tonight.

'What do I do?' I asked my friend as we stumbled foggily into the bathroom, taking a dance break from the wildness outside.

'How do I kiss her? Do I do it? Is she going to do it? Do I do it in front of people?'

I'd never kissed a girl before, let alone in the middle of a nightclub.

And I'm married.

And people know who I am . . .

I'm stopped and asked for photos when I'm out and, what, I'm going to kiss a girl, right here, where anyone could see?

I didn't know how to act. I didn't know how far I could push it. Whilst this innocent flirting was most likely very common for her on a night out, the thought of just grabbing a girl's hips or dancing closely with her was completely foreign to me. Plus, she was shorter than me – something else totally new. With my husband or any guy I'd ever been with, I was always the small one. So when I was with her, taller and bigger, I didn't know what I was meant to do. Was I meant to grab her? Who plays which role here? Obviously that's a whole different conversation around gender stereotypes, but this is what was going through my head as a conventionally 'straight' woman in society.

As the night went on, the drinks flowed and her friends got bolder and bolder.

'You're *so* going to fuck!' one of them leaned in and shouted in my ear.

I balked again. No! I was married!

But I'll kiss her in the bathroom if she wants . . . I thought. I couldn't get the idea out of my mind.

Even if it didn't happen – even if that night amounted to nothing – I was still having the time of my life. I was in an environment where I felt safe, I wasn't being judged. No-one was looking at me. No one cared who I was. It was liberating.

We headed outside, on our way to another club, and as I stood waiting by the door, I heard someone shouting.

'Sharon! *Sharon!* I've got a taxi, come on!'

I looked around, wondering who the fuck 'Sharon' was and how she'd managed to miss this girl shrieking her name.

'Sharon!'

The doors opened and my crush walked out, grabbing my hand in one of hers, wrapping her other arm around my waist and holding me close as we walked down the stairs to the row of waiting cabs.

'It's Sophie, you idiot,' my crush said pointedly to the woman who'd been shouting for Shazza. The woman I met that night screaming the wrong name at me – whose name I later learnt was Harriet – is now one of my best friends in the world. She still has me saved in her phone as Sharon. Gosh, it provides us with so many laughs.

The way that my crush responded to Harriet, it was almost like she took a bit of ownership of me in that moment. It was exciting. Her hand on my lower back was electric, just like when I shook her hand for the first time over a year ago when we met on the panel. A jolt of pure energy.

The night wore on and on, and still, I wanted to make a move but I had no idea *how*.

Do I just kiss her?

Do gay people just openly kiss other gay people?

Surely, she'll kiss me. She's the gay one, right?

Does she even want *to kiss me? Or is she just liking this attention?*

She was playing with me, whispering in my ear, pushing her body up against mine as we were dancing, putting her head on my shoulder, doing everything she knew would make me quiver. And I couldn't get enough.

Our group of eight was down to four when Amelia, who'd been my wing woman all night, decided she needed to head home. Which meant I had to go too. We live around the corner from each other and I'd arrived with her, so if she was going to go, I was clearly going to with her, as it was the safest option for us both. It was nearing 5am . . . and whilst Amelia insisted it was time for her to go, she urged me to stay. To keep enjoying myself and to see where the night took me.

By 5am, the club was closing. There were three of us left – me, my crush and one of her friends – and we made our way out of the club, daylight threatening to break through the dimness of dawn any second. We were drunk, all of us – but her other mate was poleaxed.

'Sooo are you two going home together or what?' she slurred.

We looked at each other, not sure what to say, the tension between us set to explode any minute.

'Can you please just kiss so we can all go home? You obviously like each other. Just hurry up.'

Awkward, although she wasn't wrong.

'No, we're not going to kiss,' my crush replied. 'I can't. She's married.'

There it was. The reason she hadn't made a move in the club was exactly what I'd suspected. It wasn't that she didn't want to, but she had no interest in being the 'other woman'.

I turned to her, holding my breath, ready to confess.

'It's fine. Jaryd knows everything. Trust me.'

Her friend took the hint, jumping into a cab as we stood there on the pavement staring at each other, sinking into that exquisite 'will-we-or-won't-we' feeling, neither of us prepared to make the first move.

'I need to be completely honest with you,' I started. 'You obviously know how I've felt about you. It's been a very badly kept secret for a long time. Yes, I'm married. But Jaryd is across everything and he supports it and . . .'

'I just don't want to get involved in something . . . I don't want to disrespect anyone,' she interrupted.

She was so torn – I could see it all over her face. She obviously wanted me, but she also really liked Jaryd as a friend and didn't want to do anything to disrupt their friendship either. And for all she knew, I could have been bullshitting, telling her it was fine with him when he actually had no idea. I understood exactly how confronting this situation may have been for her, so I stepped back, both physically from her, and mentally from the idea of kissing her.

'That's totally fine, I respect that. Thank you for being honest,' I said.

'I'm going to give you a kiss on the cheek now,' she said to me, 'and I'm going to jump in that taxi behind me. We're going to leave it for tonight and we'll reassess . . . later.'

After all that, it's not going to happen.

She leaned in close and slowly, softly, pressed her lips to my cheek, at the very corner of my mouth. If I'd moved barely an inch, her mouth would've been on mine, warm, soft, sensuous. She was trying to do the right thing – she didn't want to get involved with a married woman – but she was dying to kiss me as well.

She pulled back, only a little, and I could feel her breath on my cheek.

'Don't you dare kiss me there,' I whispered in her ear.

Not if you're not going to kiss me properly.

And then she did.

She grabbed me and kissed me – and it was the most intense kiss I'd ever experienced.

It should have been strange – I was kissing a girl for the first time – but it wasn't. It was everything that I had built up to be; it was intense, it was seductive, it was passionate.

It was five in the morning and I was making out with a girl, pressed up against a bin in the middle of the busy street, people spilling out of clubs everywhere after their nights out. Very quickly, I forgot all about the fact that I was married; that I was a mother, that I was Sophie Cachia.

In that moment, that's exactly what I wanted to be doing.

And I did not care what anyone thought.

Chapter 10

Things went from zero to 100 after my first kiss with *her*. Suddenly, it was like I had a girlfriend *and* a husband. I'd wake up to messages wishing me good morning, texts saying things like, 'Hey, beautiful, when am I going to see you again?'

'Did you have a good day?'

'When do you want to catch up?'

'I want to have sex with you . . .'

Our texts to each other as we made our way home after our first kiss were pretty steamy. She'd pulled herself away from me that night and jumped in a cab, without saying a word, but the floodgates had opened (literally) and it all went next level.

'I want your hands on me,' I'd written to her, one of many overtly sexual texts that flew back and forth between us as we drove away from each other. 'I'm coming to your house right now.'

'No,' she'd said. 'If we're going to do this, I don't want you to be drunk.'

I appreciated her thoughtfulness and her ability to have respect for me in such a tense moment, but fuck, where did she get that restraint?

We kept texting, calling, flirting, spending more and more time together, and Jaryd was still across it all. He knew when we were talking. He knew when we were meeting up for a coffee. He knew everything and, as far as he was telling me, he was fine with it.

Was he actually fine with it, though?

I often found myself wondering. He would tell me that he felt no jealously, no competitiveness and no ego because she was a woman. He wasn't threatened in the same way he would be if it was a male that I was having this amount of communication and connection with. Looking back, I do believe that he was as naive as me in these moments. Though both well aware that we had been facing some separate relationship issues over the past year, neither of us would have imagined that this could possibly turn into something more meaningful. To me, it was having fun and it was harmless. I hadn't been in this position with a female before, so I was unaware of the change in me that this would bring.

I'm still straight.

I just want to experience life a little bit.

I'm straight.

I just want to have sex with a girl.

But I'm definitely straight . . .

I was also loving getting to know her friends. I had been welcomed with open arms by this group of people and a whole new and different world was opening up to me; a world of acceptance where there was no judgement and no pressure to fit a mould forced onto us by bullshit archaic societal norms that have been in place for hundreds of years. I'd seen a glimpse of this new world that night at the club, with her friends, and the more I ventured into those relationships, the more I was finding my place in the world. I didn't realise that's what was happening at the time, but this was the start of me discovering where I truly belonged.

One of her good friends was gay, very masculine and even had a bit of facial hair on her, something I found so intriguing. This was someone I perceived to be a woman, but she had a beard. It never came from a judgmental place – I was just fascinated by people who were so confident, who dressed and presented exactly as they wanted to in life. This person who rocked her facial hair was inspiring to me, because she was living life exactly how she wanted to.

This new group of humans I was opening up to were teaching me so much about how to be in the world, how to live my own truth and to honour my authentic self. It was a level of radical self-acceptance I'd never seen before, and while I'd always been self-assured and not prone to giving a fuck what other people thought, this was the first time I had been surrounded by other people who lived their lives that way too. It was inspiring, empowering and fulfilling – things I'd lacked in friendship circles for some time.

We went out to a netball game one night, me, *her* and two of her friends who knew about 'us'. I bought a new outfit – jeans and a cute top, because I wanted to keep it casual but also do enough to maintain her attention – and I did my hair and makeup immaculately. I wanted to look hot, for *her*. Somehow, despite being in the public eye, it all still felt so normal.

And I *liked* it.

We all went back to her place for dinner after the game. We walked into the lounge room, her friends tagging along a few paces behind, and she grabbed me and kissed me, hard.

'I've been waiting to do that all day,' she smiled as she pulled her mouth away from mine.

Guess the new outfit must've paid off...

After we ate, we cuddled up together under a blanket on the couch, watching a movie with her friends. It scared me a bit just how normal this all felt, how right, even knowing my life was back at home. Only a couple of weeks earlier, I'd never even touched a girl, let alone kissed one. Now all of a sudden I was snuggled under a doona with this woman at her home, holding hands and kissing like this was real.

It felt like I had arrived; like this was truly me, who I was meant to be.

The end of the night came, her friends left and the conversation turned to us having sex. It was pretty clear by that point that it was going to happen and we discussed it very openly. I wanted her, even though I was still beyond nervous about the idea of being with a woman. But she wouldn't do it. Not that night.

'Your first time with a woman is a really big deal, Soph,' she told me. 'I want you to enjoy it. I want you to be present.'
Sigh.

I loved that about her. I mean, I was totally sexually frustrated at this point, because I *really wanted* this, but I couldn't fault her for wanting to make sure the experience was amazing for me, for wanting to ensure I was comfortable and relaxed and feeling good. This woman was amazing – and I was completely besotted with her. To me, she was perfect – although I must admit, as much as I wanted to sleep with her, the thought of having sex with a woman, of me touching a woman, did still petrify me. I didn't think I was going to like a vagina. I liked penises, right? And I was very *good* at what I did with men.

What if I'm bad at sex with a girl?

What if I go down on her and I don't like it?

It was a problem for another day; something future Sophie would have to figure out. I left that night, sexually unsatisfied but more in love with the idea of this woman and I together.

~

Jaryd and our son Bobby's birthdays are a week apart, and every year, I'd fly them both up to the Gold Coast for a father-son weekend together. They'd go to Movie World, hang out and have fun, just the boys, and it meant I had the house to myself for a couple of nights. So I invited her over – ostensibly for dinner, but we both knew what was on the agenda. Jaryd knew, too. I wasn't trying to do the sneaky on him, he knew perfectly well what I had planned for the weekend, and he'd indicated his full approval.

She was free, so we locked it in, and the week leading up to it was the longest week of my life. I was counting down the minutes. I was just so excited, but I was terrified as well. I was about to have a girl over, have dinner and have sex with her. What the fuck was going on?! I definitely blocked out a lot of the emotions, because I knew if I consciously engaged in them too much, the reality of what was happening would become too 'real' for me.

Finally, the night arrived. It was like a date. I heard the knock on my door, raced down to find her standing there, bottle of red wine in hand. I was *so fucking nervous*. We ordered Vietnamese takeaway and sat on the couch, talking and laughing, giving flirty touches. I couldn't get out of my head – it was so normal but also so weird for me. My thoughts were giving me mental whiplash, and confusion plagued me. How I could be here, enjoying myself this much, with her?

I'm straight. Why do I like this?

But I am fucking loving this . . .

There was something about the fact that she was a woman. It was more than just a sexual connection, which I'd felt with men in the past, that I felt with my husband. It was comfort. It was a sense of relatability. It was feeling like I could really be me; fully, deeply, authentically myself. Even though I had a beautiful man who loved and accepted every part of me, every conversation with this woman – every movement, every touch – was teaching me more about myself that I never knew before.

We'd had a few wines with dinner, but we weren't drunk – not even close – and the pressure of what lay ahead of us weighed on me. I couldn't just outright ask her to come up to the bedroom . . . It didn't feel right, and this meant so much to me. But, fuck, we had to go upstairs to the bedroom at some point.

We'd been watching free-to-air and wanted to put on a movie, but Netflix wasn't working on the TV downstairs, so we needed to go up to my bedroom. I swear to God this wasn't a ploy, but it sure fucking sounded like one. I was mortified at how 'set up' this whole thing looked.

'You're going to think I'm lying, but Netflix doesn't work down here,' I said nervously. 'So we'll have to go upstairs.'

I don't know why I freaked out about asking her to the bedroom. It's what we'd planned, how we'd already determined the night would go when we'd spoken about it the week before. She would come over, we'd have a wine, we'd put a movie on and just take it from there. But suddenly I was a teenager, forgetting everything I'd ever known, rattled with nerves about the unknown I was about to dive into.

'I want you to know that it's not about me tonight,' she'd told me during one of our planning calls.

'I'm going to make it all about you as the first step. Don't feel any pressure to touch me, to do anything to me. I just want you to feel comfortable and confident first and then we'll take it from there. No expectations.'

I led her into the room I shared with my husband and sat on the bed. She was uncomfortable. 'Jaryd sleeps here,' she reminded me, as if I wasn't already acutely aware. But there wasn't anywhere else to go.

'Well, I don't really feel like having sex with you on my son's bunk beds,' I laughed nervously. 'Don't overthink it. We're just going to watch a movie.'

Take your own advice, Soph.

Don't overthink it.

But how could I not? I'd never been nervous sexually before, but then, I'd never experienced touching, affection, this level of physical intimacy with a woman, either. For the first time in so long, a sexual experience was foreign to me – suddenly, I was a virgin again at 27.

'Are you okay?' she asked.

I was shaking.

'I'm fine, I promise. Just nervous.'

I'd never even *seen* a vagina that wasn't my own, not in this sense anyway. A confronting reality, to be honest, and one I didn't know how I was going to react to. I wasn't used to feeling this vulnerable and nervous, and even though my nerves were totally understandable, I was still petrified that she'd be able to tell.

I love sex. I am *good* at sex. I love exploring and trying new things and, having been with the same person for nearly eight years, I'd become accustomed to feeling self-assured in the bedroom. But this was someone new, a woman. It was *her*, and the confidence I usually felt wouldn't come.

Thanks to my nerves, it took a long time for it to actually happen. I loved kissing her and I was getting so turned on while we were making out, but the second she put a hand on me, I'd freeze. I don't know why – it definitely wasn't because I didn't want her to. It was scarily new. I was shaking so much that she stopped more than once to check if I was okay. Was she making me uncomfortable? Did I want to stop?

No, no, no.

'Absolutely not,' I told her. 'I'm just fucking nervous.'

She'd tried to put her hand down my pants a few times and I'd felt physically sick with nerves, I nearly vomited. I'd had to sit up and she called it at that point.

'We can't do this. I can't do it.' It just wasn't in her nature to allow anything to happen unless I was completely comfortable.

I begged her to bear with me – it's what I desperately wanted, I was just so unsure of myself, so out of my comfort zone.

I also faced another 'first' that I hadn't ever given much thought to. It wasn't just the physical act of having sex that was making me edgy; when I saw her naked, I instantly felt insecure about my body. I'd never felt ashamed of how I look before, never been self-conscious or embarrassed when I'd been with my husband or other men before him. But I quickly found that, with a woman, I began comparing myself.

Oh God, my boobs don't look like that. I've breastfed babies!

My vagina looks different to hers. Ah, I've given birth twice!

She's got no cellulite . . . her legs are so soft . . . Fuck, why are mine so prickly?

She was this incredibly fit, athletic, muscular, toned super-star. And I was just feeling like some sloppy mum of two. I was damaged goods, in comparison. So while my first time with a woman was beautiful, it also definitely uncovered a lot of insecurities for me.

I tried to put it out of my mind, tried to focus on being present to the moment and everything that was happening.

'Can I take your pants off?' she asked. Always so respectful, the whole way through.

I nodded. She tugged at my jeans, slipping them over my hips. I was extremely turned on and things had gotten pretty wet downstairs.

She put her hand in between my thighs and moaned . . .

'What, what's wrong?' I was shocked by the sound she'd let out.

'My God . . . you're so fucking sexy.'

She was excited by the fact that I was so turned on. She hadn't even done anything yet, but feeling how aroused I was getting was turning *her* on. It wasn't something I'd ever really experienced with a man. Guys would get all hot and turned on when you'd touch their dick, but with her − with girls in general, I later learnt − you get more pleasure from *giving* pleasure than receiving. And it's beautiful.

'Can I please go down on you?' she asked, a pleading tone to her oh-so-respectful question.

As if I was going to say no. That's what we were there for, right? That's what girl sex was, yeah? Experience has since taught me that there's much more to it than that . . . but then, I smiled and nodded as she slowly made her way down my body. The soft, gentle, sensual touch of her tongue was blissful − not just because of the pleasure I was receiving, but because of how much she was enjoying doing it. This girl was having the time of her fucking life and I wasn't even doing anything!

If sex with a girl means I can just lay here and not do anything, I want to do it more.

But the more I got into it, the more I wanted to reciprocate.

'I . . . think I want to touch you,' I whispered, as my confidence began to build.

'No, no, I'm fine, you don't have to.'

Me touching her had never been in the plan. I'd had some friends over earlier in the day for a pep talk and I'd said to them that there was there's no way I was going to be able to touch her vagina with my mouth. Fuck no – I'm not into it. (I'm straight, remember?) But as I lay there with her mouth on me, I wanted to try . . . and I discovered very quickly how into it I was.

A woman's vulva is, without a doubt, one of the most beautiful sights I've ever seen. As someone who lived with such a deep-seated insecurity around whether mine 'looked nice' – someone who often asked herself, 'Is the colour ok? Does it have a scent? Why is that bit longer than that part?' – I instantly appreciated the female body from a refreshingly new perspective.

Insecurity about female anatomy stems from what I believe is the lack of open conversations about those body parts when we are younger. Whilst all human body parts are unique in their own characteristics, women often place more pressure on themselves to have more symmetry down there than they do their eyebrows. Despite being in a marriage where I was loved and embraced, I undertook a labiaplasty after the birth of my second child, the rawness of my childhood insecurities spurring me on to have the surgery. The operation consists of a procedure to reduce the size of the labia minora – the flaps of skin on either side of the vaginal opening. I also had some internal tears and subsequent excess skin after child-birth that was required to be removed, but the choice to have my vulva manipulated was purely cosmetic. I sit here now, having come quite literally face-to-face with a diverse range of beautiful vaginas, incredibly disappointed in my decision not to embrace my given anatomy in the way she deserved.

When we were both satisfied, we lay there into early hours of the morning, cuddling and kissing. While I felt like I was losing my virginity for the second time, I couldn't wrap my head around how different it was in comparison to the drunken sexual experiences you have when you're younger and exploring for the first time. Being so present during such a powerful experience had been terrifying, yes, but magical, and looking back, I can't thank her enough for giving me that moment in the way that she did. I was aware, I was present and I knew I felt like me.

In hindsight (and after comparing it to my later experi-ences with women) it was probably a very *generic* night of sex for her. I laugh to myself and slightly cringe thinking about it. It must have been so bad for her, but I hold her in such high regard and appreciation that she allowed me to explore and experiment with my sexuality with her.

It's quite ironic that I now look back to masturbating as a teenager and the fact that I experienced my first-ever orgasm while watching girl-on-girl porn. It was something I never would have dreamed I'd experience but something I intrinsically found appealing from a young age. The level of connection I've achieved during sexual experiences with women is nothing like anything I've ever experienced with a man. I absolutely cannot fault Jaryd as a sexual partner – he was always incredibly generous and attentive in his devotion to my pleasure – but with another woman, when two energies align, there's a level of relatability, a sameness, a collective understanding about the world and our position in it.

That night changed my world forever.

A week later, I was standing in the supermarket, looking around whilst waiting in the queue, and I noticed this tall blonde girl standing at the checkout. She had long legs, a gorgeous tan – her skin was glowing – and she had these little denim shorts on with a white T-shirt.

I wonder what her boobs look like under there.

I wonder what her pussy looks like . . .

God, Sophie, you're here to get bananas and apples and you're wondering what some girl's vagina looks like! What the fuck?

For the past year, I hadn't been attracted to women in general – it was just *her*, this one random meeting, and my blinkers were on. I wasn't gay. *I wasn't.* But after that night, after we'd had sex, I started to look differently at women as a collective.

My curiosity now applied to *all* women.

~

Considering the absolutely cataclysmic effect the first woman I was with had on my entire life, things with her ended incredibly abruptly.

We kept hanging out after the night we'd had sex – our one and only time, by the way, so I guess it must have been terrible – but it was mostly in group situations, like at sporting games, things like that. There's a bit of a running joke amongst gay girls that you always fall in love with the first girl you hook up with, but while it's a stereotype, it was actually true in this situation. And I believed I did. I actually thought I loved her.

In the weeks after we slept together, she was relying on me for some emotional support around some career stuff she was going through, and I was happy to be that support for her. We were still very emotionally entangled after that night together and still speaking a lot on the phone. Everything seemed great, but while I had certainly pictured us together, I hadn't given a lot of thought to where this was heading. I was just going with it.

As I was leaving her place one Sunday night after she'd cooked me dinner, we kissed at the door, and she asked when she would see me again. 'I'm actually pretty busy with work and the kids this week,' I replied. I was very into this girl, but I still had a business and a household to run.

'Oh what, you don't have a lunch break for me?'

'Yes, of course, give me a call on Tuesday and we'll organise something.'

'Cool, I really want to see you,' she said before kissing me goodbye again.

The next morning, I got a message from her that I did *not* see coming.

'Hey, I think we should end this, I just want to be friends.'

I'm sorry, what?

Now, look – I had to be okay with it. I was still married, after all. But what the fuck had happened after I left her place less than twelve hours earlier? She kissed me at the door. She asked to have lunch with me that week – had pushed for it when I said it might be tricky with work!

'What's wrong? I just saw you yesterday . . .' I typed back.

'Nothing, Sophie. But you're married. We just need to be friends. This is going too far.'

Out of the blue, it felt like she was putting it all on me, implying that I was making the situation more than it was; I was being 'too much'. That was the really disappointing thing because I quite simply didn't think it was fair. She had as much a part to play as I did but was acting as if I was too full-on; like it was just a bit of fun for her and I had taken it too far.

I later found out that she had met someone else (suspicion makes me wonder if she was seeing us both at the same time). They ended up dating for a while, and whilst I wasn't utterly heartbroken that we didn't end up together, I also didn't feel great that someone who had been involved in such a huge life experience for me would so abruptly pack up and leave.

She would later tell me that the whole situation became simply too much for her. That was something I could've understood if she had only told me. But my feelings were really hurt and I resented her after that – part of me still does.

As angry as I may've been, though, I can't ignore the most glaringly obvious fact: my entire life changed thanks to *her*.

Chapter 11

With Jaryd and I both having such high sex drives, our sex life was what we would both call very healthy. Like, five or six times a week, for roughly eight years straight. There were never droughts or dry spells under our roof; being active in the bedroom always came naturally to us. But from the moment I had sex with a woman for the first time, my attraction to men – not just Jaryd, all men – began to decline.

Rapidly.

It didn't disappear completely, mind you, but it certainly diminished. It was women I craved, women I would look at when I was out, women I would think about when I was home alone, in the shower, turned on. Jaryd could feel it, too. He could sense it.

One of my best friends, Georgie, told her mum – who's gay – about the kiss I'd shared with this woman outside the club that morning.

'Tell Sophie to be careful,' she'd told my friend. 'Because she won't go back.'

Whatever, this is just fun. I love my husband!

But she was insistent.

'If she genuinely wants her relationship with Jaryd to work out, she needs to stop this – and stop it now.'

At the time, I laughed it off. I was exploring, I was in my twenties, I was having a bit of fun.

But she was right. Oh, she was right.

It was horrific to accept – something I still struggle with to this day – the realisation that my interest in my husband, this man who I still loved so dearly, was waning. People will say, 'Well, that's the choice you made' – and, yes, it is; but I was following my intuition. Did I ever, in my wildest dreams, think that sleeping with this woman, as a life experience, would result in me falling out of love with Jaryd? This sincere, attentive, loyal person, this devoted father of my children, who I thought was the sexiest man to walk the earth, with whom I shared the best relationship . . . did I ever *actually* think that I'd fall out of love with him? No. Not for a second.

But it wasn't as simple as that. I loved him, yes. So much. But there were things happening in our relationship at the same time, bubbling away beneath the surface, that nobody knew about – not to mention a whole lot of shit happening within me that I was grappling with personally. So, while it's easy enough for people who are on the outside to look in and assume that we split up because I realised I liked women – and yes, absolutely, that was part of it – Jaryd knows and I know that we had other issues that we were contending with long before *her*.

No-one had done anything wrong or bad, but we'd been together since we were barely 20 years old, and that is really young in the context of life. We'd had a baby when he was 21 and I was 22. We got married at 24 and 25, had our second baby at 25 and 26. We'd done a hell of a lot in our twenties. Everyone thinks that because I have had multiple partners since we split, that it was me who called time on our relationship, but we mutually decided to separate. Jaryd was also in a marriage that he didn't want to be in and he, too, felt a suffocating amount of pressure throughout this period.

Do we intentionally seek out change? Or is it a naturally occurring part of life? You can easily argue both sides. But with any change comes ramifications, which have a snowball effect on our future. It's fair to assume that we'd all like change to be positive; ideally, it would always take us to a place of higher value or deeper satisfaction. But that's not always the case. It's common to fear change, to fear the unknown, however after going through the huge process I did, I can now look at it with nothing but acceptance. I can embrace it as a period in which your future is only just being created. Change, over the years, has allowed me to reveal unknown strengths, passions and an entirely new version of myself I didn't know existed. Jaryd has, too. The process of change was something that, while not always easy, was relatively smooth as both our already open minds had readied us to be fluid in this situation. It was a natural progression of what we had always known in our lives together.

~

I suffered horrific postnatal depression after Bobby was born and it manifested as both social and separation anxiety. I couldn't be away from him, not even for a night. I was diagnosed with Generalised Anxiety Disorder, characterised by irrational thoughts that if I went out anywhere, I would die, and Bobby would be left without a mum. I'd never felt the sense of both love and worry I experienced when I become a mum. Being so young, my only real concern in life prior to being responsible for someone's life was whether or not my uni assignment was going to be submitted on time, or how long was left in my shift at work on Sunday. I recall sitting with my mum at the doctor's office – one of many times a family member had to take me in there themselves because I couldn't drive – and asking her, 'When will I stop being so worried?' with a tear rolling down my face.

'Never,' she said. 'You just get more used to it.'

Jaryd took me out to the local movies one night, where I suffered a panic attack because we were seated in the middle of a row and I couldn't handle not being able to get out if the roof collapsed on me. I would have panic attacks in the car if I got stuck in traffic or the light stayed red for too long – the cars around me made me feel claustrophobic. Even going out for dinner was terrible. If the lighting was dim and I was at a busy restaurant, I'd panic that I wouldn't be able to see clearly if a fire started and the place went up in flames. And don't even start me on going to the MCG to watch a footy game one evening – that was obviously the night I was certain there would be a terrorist attack and we'd all die in a brutal bombing. These highly irrational thoughts consumed me for many months, resulting in an exhausted mother who wasn't being the best she could for her baby, her husband and most importantly, for herself.

If I had to go out and have Bobby stay at Mum's, I'd have an anxiety attack because I wasn't by his side. Things got so bad that I couldn't sleep unless he was sleeping in the bed next to me and I ended up going on medication to help me with that, and to get my sleep back to a somewhat regular pattern.

After Floss was born, in January 2017, I began to internally struggle with my identity again.

What the fuck had I done with my life? I had two kids, and I loved them so much that it hurt my soul. Being a mum is what I was *made* to do. I was a brilliant mother, and it came very naturally to me. But as a *woman* – as Sophie – I was watching all my friends go on these wild adventures, doing Contiki tours, packing up and moving overseas with exciting job prospects . . . and it pains me to admit it, but I was having this moment of . . . I guess I'd almost call it regret. For the first time since becoming a mother at 22, I was overwhelmed with the sense that I was mourning a life I hadn't experienced.

My mental health was much better with Florence than it was with Bobby, her being my second child, but still, I'm their mum, I'm always going to be connected to them by a rope. I've had friends who have had kids and still gone overseas, gone off on trips, and they've been perfectly fine to leave their kids at home with Nan while they travelled. I didn't judge these people for doing this, for enjoying some alone time. I *envied* them because I believed I'd never be able to do it.

I remember crying to Jaryd, explaining that I was missing a part of me that I felt had died when I became a mum.

'But you *can* do all of those things, Soph,' Jaryd would say to me. 'I'm fully supportive of you doing that. The kids will be fine here with me.'

I knew that I could. *Of course* I could. It wasn't a question of whether I could *physically* go or not, whether Jaryd would support me, if he'd be okay with the kids on his own. It was psychological. I couldn't go – not because the kids would struggle without me, but because I knew I'd be anxious about being so far away from my children, and it wasn't worth the risk of feeling like that.

So, there I was, struggling with this very deep, tempestuous identity crisis. I had always been such a brave, independent person, and somehow becoming a mother had made me soft. I felt like I was on the verge of a mental breakdown, day after day, and the pressure I was feeling combined with the guilt of being a 'bad mother' was suffocating. One of my most painful memories is of watching Bobby as he slept one night when he was a baby, my innocent, chubby-faced angel, while I sat there crying and apologising.

'I'm sorry Mummy is crazy, baby. I'm sorry. You didn't sign up for this.'

I was in tears, convinced that the images I'd conjured in my mind of being confined to a psych ward, wrapped in a straitjacket, would soon become my reality.

Jaryd struggled with his own demons for quite some time, too, and I spent years and years trying to get him to understand that. It was brutal to watch someone who had worked so tirelessly, busting his ass and doing everything he possibly could to fulfil his potential within the AFL, have his dreams end so abruptly. After four years, the fantasy he'd had since he was a little boy was bluntly cut short – and he was lost with how life now looked for him. As his partner, I was completely shattered for him; devastated that, regardless of his natural talent and commitment to the sport both physically and emotionally, he was told he wasn't good enough. It was over for him. I saw the pain, the confusion; he was a lost little boy who now didn't know what to do. So I did anything and everything I could to assist him and to help him find happiness yet again. To help him find his place.

I agreed to move to Adelaide so he could go back and play with friends in the SANFL – where we, as a family, could just be us for a while and get everything back on track. I regularly signed him up for short courses that he'd tell me he was interested in, supported his enrolment in a uni course, smiled and nodded every time he would start a new job. But just like he did with all those courses, he would quit after a few months because he didn't like it.

He was forever seeking happiness but was never content because he was still mourning a career and a life he had also lost, through no choice of his own. I would assure him that it was okay if he needed help. That it was okay if he, in fact, was not okay. That there was a much bigger picture at play here – his role as a father, one he was so bloody brilliant at – and that his son was more important that any game. But Jaryd is proud – so damn proud – and he could never bring himself to admit his mental struggles. It became damaging for him, for me and for our family dynamic.

He had always helped me through my mental health struggles and I continually tried to understand how I could best support him, too. I left no stone unturned, booking him into psychologists' appointments and even ringing his parents to let them know exactly how bad he was at one stage. Why was nothing I was doing helping? Why did he go to his doctor twice and then cancel the rest of his appointments? Why did he laugh at the thought of being put on medication? Why did he continue to tell his dad he was happy, knowing he was lying?

It is no secret that mental health battles are horrific, and some of my own experiences I wouldn't wish upon my worst enemy. Yet not a lot of discussion exists around how fucking debilitating it can also be to try desperately to support someone who doesn't want help. For years, I lived with someone I'd constantly embrace, validate, support and attempt to motivate, all while trying to stay afloat in my own new role as a mum. I was selfless in that time, but of course, I needed to be – this was my beautiful husband letting go of himself every day before my eyes. But I had no options left. I felt like I'd exhausted every tool I had and I had to accept that I could no longer help Jaryd if he didn't want to help himself – but doing so has forever left a scar on my heart.

~

I believe something was triggered in me when my daughter arrived in 2017. Looking back now, I can see that when

I birthed Florence, I also birthed *her* – my true self – at the same time, because my whole world changed that year. During those months I was grappling with my identity crisis whilst simultaneously developing a growing obsession with the stunning blonde I'd met that fateful night at the AFLW event, I was also facing some home truths about my darling husband.

Jaryd is a beautiful man. He's so accepting, so generous to everyone in life . . . just so bloody *nice*. I cannot fault him in his kindness and his nature. He really was a wonderful husband in many ways – the kind of husband that many would dream of. What I found most attractive was that he was also a natural father. He also took on a lot becoming a dad at just 21, and still to this day, I am so proud of him for embracing it with such enthusiasm. Proud of both of us, as a team. We were a couple for almost a decade, since our teenage years, and during this time we had two gorgeous children and got married smack bang in the middle of it all.

But when it comes to everyday things, like finances, career, paying the bills, home organisation, life admin – 'being an adult', I call it – he's slack. Worse than bad, and I know he will laugh at this because even he agrees.

Believe me when I say it was really fucking difficult to separate from someone who's so damn *nice*. Someone who treated me well and who didn't cheat; someone who treated me with respect and was a great dad. But while 'nice' is great, 'nice' doesn't always make the best partner. Nice is good – but is nice reliable? Does nice always support your emotional and mental needs? Nice doesn't pay the bills. Nice doesn't always drive you to constantly bring the very best out of you. I already had two children and for a long time, I felt I had a third, too.

I ran the household finances for the entirety of our relationship. Managing finances hadn't been a strength of either of ours when we met, but I learnt quickly upon co-habiting that I'd have to take the reins if it was going to get done. I knew exactly what date the mortgage was due, how much his phone bill was, what we owed for daycare each fortnight, which medical expenses we'd incurred and the exact level of health cover we were all entitled to. On occasion, to give him some responsibility, I'd hand him a bill and ask him to pay it, he'd say yes. I'd check in the next day, 'Babe, did you pay that bill?' Yeah, yeah, he'd tell me, I did. Then a month later I'd get the reminder notice.

'I thought you said you paid the bill.'

'Oh yeah, nah I forgot.'

'So, why'd you lie to me when I asked you if you paid it?'

For all of Jaryd's wonderful traits, he also had a lack of drive – something I've never publicly spoken about. Even when I was living as what felt like a caged-up, watered-down version of myself during my babies' newborn stages, I was still bursting daily with determination, passion, and the desire to really make something of myself against all odds – and I struggled to see a man with so much potential live with such complacency. It may sound trivial to some, but it was exhausting to deal with on a regular basis.

I've always wanted to flourish in whatever I was doing and becoming a young mum only made me more ambitious. I continually wanted to prove to my kids that you can make *anything* of yourself. But being so goal oriented, I have a really hard time dealing with people who say but don't do in life. I spent nearly a decade enabling Jaryd, allowing this somewhat lazy behaviour, and in the end, it burnt me out. 'Nice' wasn't enough. I needed more and I communicated that to him for years, but nothing ever changed.

People are going to think that I was being selfish in saying this; they're going to say I'm ungrateful. But why does a woman have to settle for 'nice' alone? Why was I made to feel like I couldn't want more in my life?

'You should be happy with what you've got,' people said to me while I was staring down the barrel of a separation.

But why?

I deserved more.

I can tell you now, on the other side of it all, that 'nice' is perfect to have a co-parenting relationship with. Jaryd and I have the best thing going now. If I need a favour, if I need him to pick up the kids, or if I've left Bobby's jacket at his place, he's there in an instant. But I needed more than 'nice' in a forever partner.

'You outgrew me,' he told me more than once after we split. 'I needed to do more. I needed to be better, and I couldn't give that to you.'

And I couldn't disagree. It was so unfortunate, so sad, because I loved him and he loved me – and I still do to this day. In a different way, obviously, but I do love him. He is my family and he always will be. But he needed to separate, too, to find his own happiness. Embracing fatherhood and the commitment of a marriage was second nature to Jaryd, but he needed to be alone in order to soar; to blossom into the real Jaryd Charles Cachia.

I never wished to fall out of love with him. And I live with such guilt – even now, after being separated for nearly three years – that I broke all the promises I made to him on our wedding day. But I wasn't being empowered within my relationship or my home, and towards the end of our marriage, I constantly had to look to myself for my inspiration. Jaryd knows how much guilt I still hold; guilt he says I don't deserve to feel. Even now, when we discuss these times, I cry hysterically, wondering if there was something more I could have done to hang on.

This year, Jaryd was diagnosed with Inattentive ADHD, a form of attention deficit hyperactivity disorder that can manifest in a limited attention span, lack of focus, procrastination, and being easily distracted and forgetful.

It's been so nice to see him finally gain some clarity around his life and the behaviours he's experienced his entire life.

All I would ever want for Jaryd is complete happiness and it's been great to see that this diagnosis and the subsequent work he's now putting in to understand it further has allowed him to accept parts of himself that have frustrated him for so long.

Chapter 12

Even after Jaryd and I decided to separate, I was still looking after him. We continued to live together for around twelve months because we wanted a smooth transition for the kids, and we were kind of trialling things out at first. Ending our marriage isn't a decision we made lightly, and we weren't prepared to leap into it without careful planning. Only three or four close friends knew at the time, but we actually rented a two-bedroom apartment in 2019 as a way to test the whole separation thing. Our focus was always the children – we wanted their lives to be unimpacted, for them to know no different than their usual family life. So together, we agreed to lease a separate property that we would share usage of. That way, the kids stayed put at home, and we would alternate between who stayed at the apartment solo and who stayed in the house with the kids. We liked that the separation didn't seem too brutal and cut-throat that way; that it wasn't a case of someone moving out and it being so final. We liked the idea of the 'soft separation', whereby we were able to come and go as freely as we liked, also allowing for change of mind with fewer potential ramifications.

We set up the apartment together, ordering new beds and furniture, and just like our dynamic now, there was no set routine as to who went there and when. We were each entitled to stay there, generally rotating every second weekend and during the week. If someone felt like they needed a break or wanted some alone time – they headed to the apartment. We'd tell the kids Mummy or Daddy was at work and we never even told our own families about our living arrangements.

This apartment not only allowed us each to have our own space and the ability to see other people, but also helped slowly transition the children into a life where they'd be spending time with just one parent at a time, rather than living as a whole family unit. As we always had in the past, we maintained respect for one other and our privacy, never asking questions or probing into each other's private lives, and it worked perfectly for us.

After ten months of trialling the separation, we had made peace with the fact that we would be going our separate ways permanently – another sign of how Jaryd and I have always been able to maintain honest, open communication, even through the most challenging of experiences. It was time to announce our separation.

But let me tell you, breaking up in the public eye is really fucking hard.

Leaving the 'nice guy' and then going on to date people of the same sex as you while the world's eyes are on you is even harder – especially when people don't have a clue what's going on behind closed doors.

Jaryd and I had always shared a lot of our life together online, but there was obviously a lot that the public had no idea about. It's crazy to me that people think they know your life – all the ins and outs – from the few minutes a day you share on your Instagram stories. So many people think they know your entire truth, based on assumptions and 30-second clips.

The online community saw all the fun, beautiful parts of my life with Jaryd, and that's the couple they fell in love with – the public version of us. They felt like they knew us intimately, which made announcing our separation even harder. When you reveal something like that after welcoming the public into your life – even if it's not your entire life – they feel like they're owed some sort of explanation.

Before we announced it publicly, we obviously told our families. We decided to write a joint text to send out to everyone. It sounds a bit weak but it was how we wanted to do it – to let everyone know all at once, and to put it all into one message so we weren't making a bunch of calls or sending heaps of texts.

'We're honestly fine,' we shared. 'We cannot stress to you enough how good we are. This is something we've been deciding for a while, for over twelve months, not something we just decided last week. Please respect us and this decision. And if you want to talk, please call us, we're not going to ignore you.'

It was a *huge* shock for everyone. Well, almost everyone. One of my sisters was aware that we were separating for a while, and I'd told my dad that something was going on. I hinted to him that there were going to be some changes and I told him I needed him to be accepting – which he was.

'As long as everyone is okay, I'll be here,' he'd told me.

So, my dad and my sister knew that the split was coming, as well as Jaryd's stepmum, who I'd confided in six months prior. Yet for everyone else, it would have appeared to have come totally out of the blue. Everyone thought we were so good, that we were so happy. Jaryd and I were the couple who always got along better than anyone, so no-one could believe that we would split up. The truth was, we were good, we were so happy – we just simply were not going to do that *married* anymore.

My mum – who at times had been quite old-school – was actually great with the situation. She invited me around, which was very unlike her, and asked to talk.

'What's happened?' she asked, sitting me down and handing me a cup of coffee. 'No matter what, I'm here for you. And it's obviously your decision, but I'm really upset. I thought you and Jaryd were solid.'

Well, Mum, so did I.

Once I explained to her the issues we'd been going through, our real-life marital issues, she understood – though she admitted she was very sad about it.

But Mum also saw my sadness. The broken heart of a girl who'd fallen out of love with someone she actually never wanted to fall out of love with.

By this stage we'd also publicly announced on Instagram – after months of speculation – and the newspapers and magazines were having a field day guessing at why we'd 'really' split. It seemed that everyone was hoping there was some scandal; they were prying, waiting for one of us to spill. The fact that there were rumours about my sexuality already doing the rounds only added fuel to the fire; everyone thought they knew the 'truth' and everyone thought they were entitled to an instant explanation.

'Who cheated on who?'

'Who has a new partner?'

'Is one of them gay?'

'Are they *both* gay?!'

Of course, it was never anything as titillating as that. We simply couldn't agree on some life issues. We couldn't come to a resolution on certain things. And we couldn't do it anymore. There were so many things that Jaryd did – and didn't do – that drove me to the brink. Shit, Jaryd probably couldn't handle me fucking crying and screaming at him anymore, either. Neither of us was genuinely happy.

People refused to believe that two adults could do this so peacefully, so when we announced the separation and then, six months later, I was dating a girl, people just *knew* that was the 'real' reason we really split. (*Eyeroll*)

It felt like the public saw us as characters in a movie and they didn't like the way our movie had ended, which made them angry. But this was real life; it was *my* life, and I couldn't live it for anyone but myself.

I even had his mum call me up one day, seeking answers because 'friends had been calling her'. I politely reminded her that it was none of her (or their) business who I was having sexual relations with and asked whether she was questioning her son about the same thing.

Now, if people ask me whether I'm gay these days, I actually never say, 'Yes, I'm gay,' because I don't want to stick myself into a nice little packaged box. All I know is now I'm in a relationship with a woman. I'm very attracted to females, physically, emotionally, and spiritually – so what does that make me? I've been with men, I've been with women, but what if I date a guy again one day? What if my relationship didn't work out and I then went on to date a man? Why do we need to label things? Why can't we just allow people to live and explore life? Once upon a time, I thought I knew who I was, and yes, that was me at that point in time, but when I started exploring, I discovered a different me, and I'm so excited to keep growing and learning more about who I am.

No-one wanted to believe that we were okay and that our relationship had just simply run its course. I'm sure to this day people still don't believe it, to be honest, and I couldn't give a shit. But when I had family questioning me, both to my face and behind my back, that cut a little deep.

They couldn't believe what we'd told them; as if they thought I *had* to be lying. That Jaryd mustn't be okay with it. How could a man possibly be fine with his ex-wife dating a woman? How could he possibly support her in that? They were almost digging around for the cause of the fight, the reason for this 'falling out', because then it would make sense to them. The fact that we'd separated without any drama or anger, that we'd figured it out ourselves – they couldn't wrap their heads around it, or the fact that I was dating and that Jaryd was okay with it.

He would tell me everything they said about me. He still does, because to this day, we are best friends.

'Are you okay? I saw that *Daily Mail* article about her "wanting to fuck women",' he recalled his mum saying once, telling me that he'd told her I had never even spoken to the publication.

'Oh, well, there were quotes from her in there,' his mum had said – never mind the fact that they were taken from an interview I did on a podcast three months earlier (which Jaryd also told her).

'Well, that's fine,' he'd said to her. 'But that's going to affect your relationship with your grandkids because I need you to be okay with Soph, so that if she needs you to pick up the kids from school because she's running late from work or something, I need you to be able to say yes. This is going to affect everyone and I'm not going to let it happen.'

I still cry over it – I sobbed hysterically to my girlfriend on my son's last birthday because he was another year older, and I was and am still weighed down with so much guilt that I've taken our family dynamic apart.

One positive that I believe came out of the backlash and public interest around our split was that I think it made me a better person. It made me even more accepting and nonjudgmental of other people's private situations. It's funny, Jaryd and I are always the people that our friends call when they want an unbiased opinion, a vent, or a shoulder to lean on, because they know neither of us have a judgemental bone in our body. If someone I know breaks up with their partner, I'm not interested in the gossip, I don't want to dig around to uncover some scandal. All I think is, 'I hope they're okay', because I know how tough it is, especially when you live your life in the public eye. Having experienced what it's like to be gossiped about, speculated on, to hear such fabricated versions of events about your marriage and your sex life plastered all over the news-papers and in morbid gossip forums, I'm more accepting than ever of this idea that you never know what someone's going through. Everyone deserves happiness in life – and that includes me and you.

The proof I needed that we'd made the right call for both of us came when Jaryd and I were invited as a couple to his best friend's wedding in Mexico in December 2019, not long after announcing our split. I told him he should go with his brother and I'd stay here with the kids. He hadn't been overseas in ages and it was his best mate who was getting married, so it made sense that he would go. It didn't feel right that we go together at that point, regardless of how amicable everyone knew we were. This was his moment and I needed to let him go on his own.

'Go for two weeks,' I told him. 'Go to New York while you're over there, too.'

He couldn't go all that way and not make a proper trip of it, I encouraged him.

In the photos I later saw from that trip, I saw a smile on Jaryd's face I hadn't seen in years. He was himself in those moments; he was back to being Jaryd Cachia, travelling NYC with his brother . . . living again. Although the emotion from announcing our separation was still fresh, I could not have been happier. I could tell he was starting to come back, and this is when I knew that, for the both of us, life was only just beginning.

Chapter 13

I think I was a feminist before I even knew what feminism was.

Why are we conditioned to believe that we can't be happy unless we have a partner? That if one is alone – even by choice – that they are not complete?

When Netflix released *Bridgerton* – a story of love, wealth and passion in Regency-era England – I was riddled with both anxiety and frustration at how relatable some of those storylines were to practices that somehow still exist today. Set back in the early 1800s, *Bridgerton* centres around 'debutantes' – young girls dressed beautifully, paraded around a court so that they can find a husband. Or, more specifically, so that the men can handpick their bride – with little to no say from the women themselves. Women were considered successful if they were lucky enough to be chosen to be a wife and would heap gratitude and praise on the suitor and his family.

It made me sick that, 200 years later, the message that a woman should show gratitude towards a man for the 'honour' of giving you his love is still prominent, if more subtle these days. I am disgusted that, as a seventeen-year-old, I'd partaken in what my school called a 'Debutante Ball' – a 'coming out' party for the young ladies of society, to be presented to the public wearing long, flowing white dresses as a sign of purity, innocence and virginity. At the time I partook in my Deb Ball, I had no idea what it really meant or that the practice has its roots in rituals from hundreds of years ago, when women were basically sold off to the highest bidder (and were pitied, even shunned, if no man wanted them).

Author Glennon Doyle unpacks this theme of gratitude in her book *Untamed* brilliantly, dissecting this notion that women are always told how grateful they should be in life. If you find a man that loves you and is nice enough to marry you, be grateful. If you have kids and you are blessed with motherhood, please . . . be grateful. And definitely do not ask for more. Yet, something I discovered over the years is that you can be both grateful *and* unsatisfied simultaneously. Being grateful does not mean you need to settle. You can absolutely be thankful in life and still not be satisfied, whether that's in your relationship, friendships, parenthood or career.

I was told to be grateful because I had a nice, kind husband. One who loved me and cared for me – a man that still does both of those things. As if my only purpose in life as a woman was to seek fulfillment through the way I am treated by another human. Nothing to do with what I want individually, or what my soul sought in the pursuit of happiness.

I recall chatting to Jaryd's nan one afternoon over a cuppa about a couple she knew who were splitting up. Jaryd's nan – a delightful woman, but very old-school, with traditional Catholic values.

'If anything ever happens with you and Jaryd and you think you're going to leave, come talk to me first and I'll talk you out of it,' she told me.

That's just her generation, and I will not fault her for that – she wasn't taught any different, and still upheld the notion that a successful life relied heavily on a marriage. Not necessarily a stable, loving, committed relationship, but the *title* of 'marriage' – that's what society viewed as success, presumed would bring happiness. But the times have now changed. We can be taught differently, and we can teach the next generation to do things differently, too.

As a society, we like to think that we are progressive – yet the fact that Deb Balls still occur is fucking wild to me! Like seeking partners and stable commitment, women are also meant to want to have children, because that's a woman's purpose, right? And by being in a relationship, and by producing babies, you will find yourself in a position of utter bliss and fulfillment – correct? Ludicrous.

It's always been natural to me to want something other than what society tells me. I tried to 'want' my marriage to work; I tried to 'want' to fit that mould – but it was just never me. I've never been wired that way.

Men can face the same expectations, too, though to a lesser extent. It's often assumed that guys aren't happy until they settle down, either. I've been asked so many times since our split if Jaryd had a girlfriend. I'd tell most people – well, first of all, I don't discuss his business – but if it was family or close friends asking, and I said that he *wasn't* seeing anyone at that time, their instant reaction was always the same. 'Ooh, I hope he meets someone soon to settle down with.' It never occurred to them that maybe Jaryd did not *want* a partner at that stage; that he might be happy being single at that moment in time. It certainly wasn't that he *couldn't* get a partner – I can assure you that Jaryd has never had any issues in this department. He could have had ten different girlfriends by now if it's what he wanted. But it wasn't.

Breakups, too, are viewed with so much negativity, but why does a split have to indicate a failure? Yes, it can be terrifying, heartbreaking and soul destroying to say goodbye to someone, even knowing you don't want to be with them anymore. But if two people aren't their best selves when they're together, how is their being apart a bad thing?

I know that people look at me and Jaryd and say that we 'failed' because we separated after a few years of marriage. But explain to me how on earth we failed. We have two beautiful children together – the most devoted big brother to a hilariously talented little girl with whom we've created a wonderful life. Jaryd and I have shared a strong bond for more than a decade, and now we co-parent and raise two children together, children we are immensely proud of and who we are raising to understand the importance of self-worth and life fulfillment. I got to have my children with my best friend on this earth. Where is the failure in any of that?

Ask yourself, how many 'married' couples do you know that are actually fucking miserable?

My parents stayed together well over a decade longer than they should have merely because that's what you were 'supposed to do'. I saw my dad living in complete denial and my mum becoming more miserable day by day, and it led to us living in an incredibly difficult environment for many years. More so for me because, as I was the youngest of four, my sisters had all moved out by the time things got really bad between Mum and Dad.

At the time, I used to wonder why Mum was so mean to my dad. Why she lived with such bitterness, such resentment towards him – as far as I saw, he loved her and was happy. After becoming an adult and experiencing my own relationship breakdowns, though, I suddenly found myself sympathising with my mum. Complacency wasn't enough for her. Love wasn't enough. 'Nice', funnily enough, was also no longer enough. My mum had sacrificed her entire career to be a stay-at-home carer for us four girls. To pack up the house and move interstate every time my dad got a new job. To live the traditional housewife life in order to support my dad's career. But over the years, that life wore her down. She became exhausted; unfulfilled perhaps, a lioness in a cage, bursting to be set free. When her four babies were finally adults, maybe she wanted to travel? Perhaps she wanted some spontaneity? Maybe, just maybe, she was hoping that instead of going to Noosa and plonking himself on the couch in front of the cricket for two weeks straight every Christmas, Dad might ask her if she wanted to go out for dinner. Dad's complacency is what I believe drove my mum away. She no longer wanted to live how Dad thought they 'had' to. Mum had been simply trying to stay alive for too long – she was ready to not just exist, but to truly live.

My parents know their relationship breakdown impacted me as the only child that was still living at home throughout it all, but I doubt either of them understands the full effect living in that house during their marriage breakdown had on me. It's not that they fought; that was only for the first few years. What was worse later down the track was living under the same roof as them, knowing they didn't even seem to care about the other's existence anymore. It was hard to watch and process as a teenager.

When my sisters and I had babies of our own, we'd all regularly meet at Mum and Dad's for family catchups. Unfortunately, as time went on, the tension became so thick that none of us wanted to visit anymore. We didn't want to be taking our children into such a negative space. The day they actually separated was a huge relief – a 'halle-fucking-lujah, let's throw a goddamn party' type of moment.

How does society deem that situation 'successful', simply because a marriage certificate is still intact?

A friend of mine who is in her late twenties has recently gone through a breakup with her partner of three years and she says her life is falling apart – but I look at the situation and know that her life is only just starting. How exciting, to be 27 and have your options completely open to you! She doesn't want to get married and she doesn't want to have kids, so other than not having the company of a partner, how can this be a negative thing? My friend can look back and acknowledge that they spent a great three years together, that this woman played such an important part of her life for that time, and she can take all the beautiful parts of that relationship with her forever. But now, she gets to live out her new future, and the world is her absolute oyster. It's disappointing that, at 27, we're told we should be starting to get married, settle down, think about kids ... so in her mind, she was failing at life.

Now, I'm not naive to the fact that my ability to live my life the way I want was hugely helped by having a very understanding partner in Jaryd. That's why I married him, because we're very similar in our views on life, and I can tell you right now, we'll be telling our children not to be in relationships, not to get married, unless it's what they truly want. I will be pushing my kids to have as many sexual partners, as many life experiences as possible, to travel, to try new jobs, to do anything that allows them to make the best decisions for themselves and themselves only. The only message I will push on to them is *not* to do what society expects of them if it's not what they wish. Their only 'expectation' is going to be to get the most out of life and to do what they want to do. That's what I am teaching my children: that they don't have to fit the mould that society offers us.

It took me a while to fully embody this realisation, but I'm still only 31. I'm not the brave, inspirational person that a lot of people out there apparently see me as. For me, it's quite simple, really. I certainly don't think that I'm doing anything out of the ordinary by *not* doing what's ordinary. I'm just a 31-year-old woman who wants to live her life a little bit. A woman who is prepared to take a risk, to make a couple of mistakes on the way, and to figure out what is going to suit me best.

Some people criticise my desire to always seek more, or they say I'll never be happy because I'm not content with anything I've ever had, but that's not true. I love my life and I love who I am as a person, but I'm also conscious of the old saying that I have one life in which to do as much as I possibly can. And that goes for my career as well as my personal life. I'm annoyed at myself for not achieving certain things by the time I turned 30, so now I'm focused on what I can achieve by 35. What can I achieve by 40? I want to learn and constantly be evolving.

When I bought into a hairdressing salon company, people said, 'But you don't do hairdressing.' No, I don't – but I'm learning about the business. I want to develop myself and my skills in so many different fields and I can't fathom doing the same job my entire life. That's why I didn't finish my uni degree and go straight into a job that would see me sitting behind a desk for years. I've always wanted to take a different path – I'm starting to see that it's kind of been a theme of my life.

My entire life, I wanted to be a sports journalist. I wanted to report on the world stage – travelling the globe, following the Olympics, with my family back at home watching me on the TV. Never in my wildest dreams did I think I'd find myself head of separate companies. Co-founding my sleepwear and loungewear range CACHIA back in 2017 has put me in a very lucrative position financially at 31 and has significantly contributed to my independence. We have a forever-evolving, loyal following who love our brand for its affordability, its quality and the level of customer service care provided. Alongside my business partner and staff, I have watched CACHIA go from selling a handful of styles a year to now approaching its 350,000th order.

What I also couldn't have fathomed ten years ago was making a career of digital marketing via social media – and now having a minimum of five annual salaries, all from different revenue streams.

With these opportunities that I've built for myself via a 'mummy blog' I started writing at 23, I've been able to invest money into building further companies, now finding myself heavily involved in the business owner and management sector.

Once upon a time, I was stoked at being a stay-at-home housewife. It's what I wanted at the time. But as humans, we are allowed to evolve, and we are allowed to change. Whilst some would strongly view continually changing your mind as erratic and unstable, I reject the notion that changing your mind means you don't know what you want. To me, it highlights your ability to learn and evolve. You have allowed yourself to have fresh perspectives and new, creative insights.

The truth – *my* truth – is that when I picture myself at 60 or 70 years old, I don't know what or who I see! I don't know what I want that person to look like, or where their life experiences have taken them. My sisters and I have this joke (that is also kind of not a joke . . .) that I'm going to be the drunk, rich auntie who turns up to my niece's birthday party unannounced with a bottle of champagne under one arm, fluffy dog under the other, a cigarette hanging out of my mouth and some ludicrously extravagant present ready to hand off to the birthday girl. I'll have just flown in from Paris – which nobody knows until I show up, because I'll always be jet setting off somewhere on some crazy adventure, living life in the exact way I choose. The older I've gotten, and the more I've evolved as a woman, the more I've realised I'm a free spirit, ready to be swept up in the wind gusts of life and land wherever they take me.

According to society's rules, if I'm doing that, I must not be happy. I am a desperate, miserable old woman. 'Poor me' because nobody loves me; because I was 'too erratic' to settle down.

Or maybe – just maybe – I was living life on my terms. Because to me, someone doing that – without abiding by any external social pressures – is pure fucking happiness.

Chapter 14

Back in late 2018 – before Jaryd and I had officially separated – I happened to join a women's footy team. I'd had
my first sexual encounter with a female, and I was definitely
becoming aware of my increasing attraction to a wide variety
of women, but I didn't consider myself 'gay'. I was still just
exploring, as far as I was concerned, and I was very naive to
that world. I hadn't really known any gay women growing up,
apart from that one friend's mum, who had a female partner.
But in terms of my own social circles, my upbringing, my life,
pretty much everyone was straight, and it quickly became
apparent how sheltered my life had been in this regard.

I can recall being so shocked when I was told that 22 out
of the 24 girls on my new footy team were gay. 'But they

don't look gay,' I remember thinking. Obviously, I look back with both humour and frustration at how naive Sophie could make such a statement. I'd surrounded myself with these sporty, football people (previously, I would have said women, but now I know them collectively as humans, as there were some non-gendered players), who are now some of my best friends, and they were just the most welcoming humans I'd ever come across in my life. They showed me an unconditional acceptance and a genuine warmth and openness that no-one ever had before.

Now, it's not like I started playing footy and suddenly 'turned into' a lesbian, but I do think it probably contributed to my awakening because, for the first time in my life, I was put into an environment where I was actually around gay people. Spending time with them opened my eyes to new ideas, new outlooks on life, and it helped broaden my understanding of the world; to learn how sexuality can be so incredibly fluid and how, in this environment, no one felt the need to put labels on each other.

There were teammates who were studying at uni and worked at Sportsgirl on the weekend, sure, but then there was someone who owned her own landscaping company and she'd show up to training in her big chunky work boots. There was one person who worked in the mines, a single mum of four kids, and one with half of their head shaved who rode their Harley to the oval.

Playing local footy really did bless me with the honour of meeting such interesting, unique characters – ones who I'd never have been lucky enough to meet if I never played that sport. I was associating with, socialising with, playing with and now friendly with humans I'd been so sheltered from my entire life.

I was even more inspired not to stay in the lane I'd been told to keep to my entire life – that I could step further outside the social rules that I grew up with and continue to forge a new path. I felt respected for my life choices and I felt safe to be myself, authentically and unapologetically.

I felt so welcomed by everyone I met within the LGBTQIA+ community, and so safe to be me – even if I didn't exactly know who that was yet. I didn't have as big a profile then as I do now, but I was still known in Melbourne, and I found that when I would go to gay bars and clubs, no-one cared who I was. People weren't watching me, whispering, taking secret snaps with their phones as I'd previously found. Sure, if someone knew who I was they might just come over and say, 'Hey, love your page, have a good night' – but that was it. They'd move on. They didn't think my night out was their business, and it gave me a sense of freedom and acceptance I hadn't experienced before.

Very early on (when no-one had any idea that Jaryd and I were considering separating), I was kissing this girl at a club one night, and as I turned around, another girl tapped me on the shoulder. 'Oh hey, sorry to bother you but me and my friend, we follow you and we love you. Can we have a selfie?' And I. Fucking. Died.

She's seen me making out with another woman, is she going to tell people? Is this going to get out? Are people going to think I'm cheating on my husband?

I was freaking out. But as always, I said yes to the photo, and afterwards, she and her friend thanked me – and what she did next surprised me.

'Oh, and hey . . . it's all good,' she said as she gave me a nod, seemingly acknowledging that what I was doing in my private life was none of her business, nor did she 'care' – and she wouldn't be telling anyone.

That little moment, whilst probably insignificant to this person, cemented for me that I did want to be a part of this safe space; where no-one looked at me, no-one gave a shit who I was, and no one cared why I was there. It was liberation like I'd never experienced, an environment I'd never encountered – one where everyone's truth was accepted, regardless of what that may be. Instead of pointing the finger, being embraced with two open hands. Where the 'rights' and 'wrongs' of society were non-existent. It was a completely different realm and it didn't take me long to realise that this was exactly where I belonged.

~

The way this new group of friends treated me felt so different to how old acquaintances had – including people I'd long considered my friends. I was never the figurehead of a friendship circle, never the 'leader', so to speak; the one who called the shots, who decided where we'd go for dinner, what we'd do on the weekend . . . No, I was always on the outer. However, I *have* always been the one that all of my friends have individually come to in a crisis because they know they can count on me to provide an extremely balanced, non-judgemental view. I am the person that others call on when they need to be vulnerable, when they're too scared to show anyone else their weakness.

I've had people call me when they've had affairs or cheated on their partners, or when their partner's cheating and they're too embarrassed to tell anybody.

When friends have had babies and they're realising a week or two weeks in that they're not Betty Crocker with the cake laid out perfectly on the table, and their house is not clean anymore, and their vagina hurts, and they've got postnatal depression . . . and I have sat there and helped them breastfeed and changed their pads for them. I'm that friend that people know they can turn to, no questions asked.

I'm also the friend that won't turn you away even if we haven't spoken in six months. If you tell me you need help, I will find someone to look after my kids and I will get to your side as quickly as I can. A girlfriend rang me a week or two after giving birth and I told her I'd come around for a visit. This was someone whose house was always immaculate. You'd walk in and there'd be a freshly baked cake on the table, flowers in vases, nothing out of place. I took over some food, met the baby, and I quickly realised that something wasn't right. When I got up to leave because I had to go to work, she grabbed my hand.

'Please don't leave me,' she said with tears in her eyes. And I just knew. We didn't have to talk – I already had Bobby, I understood what she was going through. So I sat there with her and stroked her head for hours as she lay on my lap sobbing, and she just held onto me. She'd hadn't been a particularly affectionate person in the past, but she just let herself be held in those moments. She was in her rawest form, boobs out while I helped her breastfeed – this is a girl who'd always been so self-conscious growing up, who never wanted to get naked or even down to her undies in front of anyone in the fifteen years I'd known her. She was just crying, holding my hand, asking for my help and telling me she loved me. In her hour of need, I was there with her.

I turned up at her house every day that week.

'I get it,' I told her when she was struggling with severe anxiety. 'I've been there. It's horrible. But you're going to get through it. If there's one thing I can promise you, it's that you will not feel like this forever. I know that feeling where you think you're going crazy. But I promise you, it won't last.'

She wouldn't let me leave and, honestly, I didn't want to. I wanted to be there for her as much as I could. And I think, to this day, I am probably the only friend that has seen her in that state because she wouldn't let anyone else see her like that. I guess I was able to make her feel comfortable enough that she knew she could be that vulnerable in front of me because she knew I provided a safe space for her.

I have been – and still am – that person for so many people, yet I feel as though few have been that person for me, and it hurts when it seems as if people won't show up to support you in your time of need. But while it's cliched, I've come to realise as I've grown older that you only need a handful of people around you – close friends who know the real you, and who actually see you for who you are. The ones willing to show up for you in the way you've shown up for them.

However, I've also had old acquaintances who did not once acknowledge that my marriage broke down, who did not acknowledge that I was suddenly dating a woman, which I'd never done before. It was painful and embarrassing, but I didn't want to let go of any one of them, including those I'd known since I was a kid. As much as I am an individual, I did cherish being a part of such groups.

I don't blame them, but it was odd to me that, when Jaryd and I split and I started dating women, very few old acquaintances called to ask if I was okay, to see if I was coping.

At first I was in denial.

They're just busy.

They have their own lives.

They know I'm strong and I usually handle things on my own.

I have spent many years confused as to why people I thought I knew well seemed not to care about me the way I had expected them to. Nobody asked how I was feeling after announcing my marriage was over – why, because it was amicable? Nobody asked me how the kids were doing. Nobody asked whether or not, when I climbed into bed at the end of the day, I was okay.

If someone I'd known for years suddenly started dating a girl when they'd previously only been with guys, I'd be reaching out to them straight away.

'Hey! What's going on?'

'How did that happen?'

'How are you feeling?'

'Are you happy?'

What I realised is that when someone's actions make people uncomfortable, they usually don't know how to navigate it, how to talk about it. And it's not just me – this turned out to be a very common theme. I've spoken to a lot of people in my online community, to other friends who have gone through different situations but experienced the same reaction.

When you're in a group of girls and someone has a new boyfriend, everyone wants to know all about him:

'OMG! What's his name?'

'What does he do for work?'

'C'mon, can we see a photo?'

'Where does he go out?'

'Does he play footy?'

When I started dating girls, though, the questions didn't come as thick and fast. It was totally taboo within this fiercely heterosexual environment. It was as if some people I had known had blinkers on, shielding them from everything that existed outside their bubble. They hadn't been exposed to any other facets of life, any other dynamics and for them, life's trajectory was very clear cut: you grow up, you go to school, you work hard, you go straight to uni, you marry your high school boyfriend, and you build your white picket fence. So when I started to say that, actually, that's not what I wanted for my life, it may have been uncomfortable. To them, what I was doing must have seemed wrong.

I remember one time I was sitting at a cafe with a girl I was seeing and a couple of people I knew from this group walked past. One told me afterwards that they'd talked about it over their brunch – 'Oh so is that the girl Sophie's dating?' – so I knew that *they* knew I was dating girls, but still, nothing. At times we'd catch up, I'd sit there, this little excited girl, bursting to tell them my news. It might come as a surprise to some, but I'm never one to want the room to be focussed on me, and making an effort to ask questions of other people before speaking about myself is something that was instilled into me since I was a little girl. So, I'd patiently wait my turn, hanging out for my chance to have the podium. But it never came. Even the one time I handed my phone to the few interested girls down my end of the table to show them a photo of my new partner, the other end of the table went almost silent, aside from some whispering amongst themselves.

Feeling like my love wasn't something to be shared and my happiness wasn't something people wanted to know about was fucking horrible.

The sad reality is that if I was dating a new guy, it would've been a totally different story. If I had a new lawyer boyfriend, if he was older, if he drove a nice car, if he was buying me expensive gifts, they'd want to know all about him. But I was dating a nineteen-year-old (eight years my junior) very masculine gay girl and I believe that they couldn't understand that, so they simply decided not to acknowledge it. I felt humiliated on more than one occasion and I'm so mad at myself for hanging around as long as I did.

In hindsight, knowing who I am now – or, who I think I am in my rawest form – I know I have now found me. These people I once knew – they weren't bad people. I just don't think they're *my* people and I think that's okay to realise as you get older who is truly a part of your team. I outgrew some circles that I never really fitted into anyway – and when I truly found my people, they were within the gay community.

Chapter 15

When I started experimenting with girls, I never would have imagined that I'd be where I am today. If you had told me three years ago, that I was going to be in a relationship and living with a woman . . . I would have laughed in your face.

And for a while after that first sexual encounter with a woman, it was still no more than experimentation. Jaryd was still across everything that was going on, he was still encouraging me to scratch that ever-growing itch, but I was caught up in my own internal battle. Jaryd and I were still together – maybe more for appearance's sake than anything, at that point – but we were both allowing each other to go out and meet new people, to explore what was out there. I was so drawn to women, so attracted to them, but I was also pushing those feelings away, rejecting them. I was suppressing a lot of my desire.

But at some point, I couldn't fight it anymore.

Fuck it. I'm going for it.

I dated a handful of women, all of whom had something new to teach me about this world and about myself. I had a lot of fun and continued to evolve into this new version of myself, this different Sophie.

And then there was her.

In July 2019, I connected with a professional female athlete who had been introduced to me online by a mutual friend. She was living overseas, but we very quickly developed a strong connection, despite the distance, talking on the phone, FaceTiming each other, messaging constantly.

We spoke every single day for 50 days straight, until she was set to come back to Australia towards the end of the year. To some it might sound ridiculous that I could feel so strongly about someone I'd only met online, but throughout our months of getting to know each other, despite being worlds apart, our chemistry grew – as did her openness towards me.

We were going to be together when she got back, there was never any question around it – so when she was due to return to Australia, I flew interstate to meet her in person not long after she arrived.

She'd messaged me as she was boarding, sending love heart emojis and sharing her excitement at finally getting to meet, to hold hands, to touch each other, to just be together at last. But by the time she landed, something had clearly changed.

I waited to hear from her after her flight arrived, but for what felt likie forever, the screen on my phone stayed black, taunting me . . .

'Ding!'

There it was.

'Hey Sophie. I think we need to talk.'

Oh . . . this didn't sound good.

Had I missed something? Had I misunderstood? My stomach flipped, my excitement transforming into anxiety as we arranged to meet at a nearby pub.

I walked in and there she was – but she didn't seem to be the same laughing, smiling, passionate woman I'd come to love over the past several weeks.

Her eyes looked empty to me as I sat opposite her on a bar stool, steeling myself for whatever was about to come.

'I'm sorry but I need to end this before it starts,' she said simply. 'I'm not going to be with you.'

My heart shattered. We hadn't known each other long, but it felt as though this woman had a grip on my soul like nobody ever had before. I couldn't understand what had gone wrong between her boarding the plane a few hours earlier and touching down in Australia.

I was heartbroken. I walked back to my hotel, where I sobbed on the floor of my room, in utter despair, for the next three days before changing my return flight to come home early. The hotel room I'd envisaged us sharing – where, for the first time, I would feel those hands on my body – was as empty as my heart.

I couldn't believe it was over before it had even begun. This girl, this woman who had reached inside and stirred something in me from across the world, had apparently taken fifteen hours to do a complete 180 – and I had no idea why. Our connection was worth something, I thought, and it meant a lot to me. What had gone wrong?

When, a few weeks later, some friends asked me to come along to a basketball game one Saturday night, I took them up on the offer. I was still hurting a bit from what had happened, but the kids were with Jaryd, I didn't have much going on, it was something different . . . Why not?

We were in the stands, having a couple of drinks, watching the game . . .

And then there was her.

We were sitting quite far back, but this blonde woman who was rocking a high bun (another common theme in my love life, apparently) was dropping 3s like it was going out of fashion. Even with my very limited basketball knowledge, I could tell she was on her game this night.

In all honesty, it wasn't her appearance that caught my attention – even though she was obviously gorgeous. It was her skill and what I later called her 'swag' on court that I liked. She was cool, I just knew it. She moved up and down the court like no one else was there, and whilst I knew nothing about the rules, strategy or gameplay of basketball (other than getting the ball in the hoop), she stood out to me. From that early on, I was fixated on her style of ball.

When it reached half time, I asked the others if they knew who she was – at this point, simply because I thought she was an epic player and I love learning as much as I can about female sport. I checked out her Instagram and couldn't believe my eyes. If someone put down the description of my dream woman on paper, Blondie With The Bun was it. I couldn't believe my eyes.

How could someone be so perfect?

She seemed too good to be true.

Talented? Tick.

Gorgeous? Tick.

Gay? Tick.

Single? Tick.

'I have to meet her,' I told my group. 'I *need* you to introduce me to her.'

At this stage, I was still dealing with a clusterfuck of emotions after the bombshell of disappointment only a month earlier, so dating someone new wasn't something I had even considered as I was still in a bit of 'survival mode'. But, I realised, I had every right to take care of my own happiness. After all, I was single and I was free to pursue any opportunity I liked – whether that was Blondie With The Bun or anyone else. After feeling so let-down after my last romantic escapade, I deserved to take a chance.

A friend of mine who knew the gorgeous blonde player had gone to talk to her post-game, so I ever-so-casually popped over after a few minutes to introduce myself. She seemed rattled – was almost shaking – and I could tell she didn't want to be talking to us. She'd dropped her full protein shaker, the chocolate liquid spilling all over the court, and with that mishap, exhaustion from an intense game, not to mention people everywhere and the fact that she was juggling her basketball, shoes and towel in her arms, I could understand that she just wanted to get out of there. (I later found out she'd just had an encounter with her ex following their split, which was the catalyst for her behaviour after the game, and it made sense the more I learnt about their past.)

But I had done what I set out to do: I got to meet her and despite the chaos she was certainly as beautiful in real life as she was on my phone. Sweaty, puffed out, and covered in the remnants of ankle tape, she was nevertheless perfect. Looking back, it was a terrible introduction – but hey, something worked, right?

'I'm asking her on a date,' I said to my friends as we left the stadium.

In the grand scheme of things, I hadn't been dating women long at this stage – roughly twelve months at most.

First, there was *her*: the brief love-at-first-sight encounter that didn't last long but changed my life forever.

Then there was *her* – the older woman. She was in her 40s and our romance only lasted for a period of around two months, as she travelled a lot for work. It was a unique experience for me, but one I look back on with nothing but respect. The confidence I went on to have in my experiences with females, I owed all to this woman. I saw her as almost a 'teacher' – someone who I could ask all my 'silly' questions and express my concerns, because, hey, she'd been around this side of town her whole life. She let me experiment with her, she showed me certain ways to do things, she encouraged me to let go and be in the moment with my sexuality and my confidence. And whilst it was sad for me to hurt her after she gave me so much, and because I valued her so highly as a dear friend, I had also made it explicitly clear that it was never going to be something serious. She was eager to settle down in love and life, whilst I had only just found the key to open my door of exploration.

Then there was *her*: my young, fun 'toyboy', if you like. She will LOVE that I called her that! Still to this day, she is a close friend, albeit from afar. She is someone I know I will always answer the phone for when she calls, as she always does for me, in those times when we still need each other. I always credited her for her maturity. She was nineteen when we met, while I was a mother of two and eight years older than her. But something about us clicked so beautifully and I do often wonder how life would have looked if I'd met her ten or fifteen years down the track. She was also the first person my family met – both my children and my parents and sisters – and they embraced her immediately. It was easy with her. She idolised me. She was fun, and we had a great time together. I still look back on the memories of our time together and smile, and I made some lifelong friends through her.

She was a lot smaller than me but could throw me round like a rag doll and, due to her very masculine persona, she loved knowing she could dominate me when she wanted to. Other than that, she was a soft puppy dog and treated me like a queen. Neither of us wanted to fully commit to each other, which I always saw as another sign of her maturity, despite her young age – she was well aware that committing to an older woman with children wasn't going to fit her timeline either. However, we spent a beautiful nine months together – even during that three- or four-month crossover, when she knew I was awaiting the day my 'online friend' would make her appearance in Australia. She just got me. She understood me. She never tried to change me, she never tried to tame me, and for that, I thank her.

But all of these women had put the first moves on me. I was new to this world and they'd taken the initiative. Blondie With The Bun, however, was the first girl *I'd* ever wanted to ask out on a date. It was new territory for me and I have to admit, I was nervous. But she was *it*; this was *her* – the girl I knew I'd been waiting to meet.

She'd followed me back on Insta the night after the game (success!), but it wasn't until the next week when I received a few drunken DMs from her after she'd been on a boozy lunch with friends that I started to think she might be interested in me, too. She'd randomly sent me some videos – with no prior convo, mind you – and I thought, 'Booyahhh, baby – she's thinking about me!' Maybe it wasn't just the dropped protein shaker that had her rattled after that game where we met.

I wanted to ask her out, but she made me nervous – I really didn't want to stuff things up. It was a new feeling for me, if I'm honest, and I was self-conscious, too. She was drop-dead gorgeous AND epically cool – I thought she was way out of my league. So rather than being straight-to-the-point Sophie, who usually had no issues with confidence when it came to showing my intentions with either males or females, I held back – and she startled me in return. Some scarce, low-key flirting between us prompted me to attend her game again the next weekend, where she had very tastefully left me a jersey at reception with her number on it without telling me. I thought the move was veryyy smooth.

It was the statement she wanted to make, but without one word about it. I liked it.

It took me three attempts within one text conversation for her to finally say 'yes' to having dinner with me the following week. I rang my token lesbian best friends and asked them how to approach the date – I'd previously only dated quite masculine women, but this girl was very feminine, like me, and I didn't know how this dynamic worked!

Who paid? What did I wear? Would it be too much if I picked her up?

We planned to go out to dinner the following week. The sting of what had happened a month earlier hadn't left me, but I had to move on and when the night of our first date rolled around, I was excited.

Earlier in the day, I'd sent a message to the one who, just weeks earlier, had semi-broken my heart – which was healing nicely by this point – wishing her good luck with an injury she'd sustained. She'd badly hurt herself and it was courteous for me to wish her well, I thought. I'm always someone who can put issues aside in 'bigger picture' moments. We got to chatting and it was friendly; it was nice. There was no animosity in these conversations, and I felt no residual hurt. I tapped out of the chat, telling her I had to go – I was about to go on a date.

Blondie and I talked for hours at dinner and I discovered she was a kind, gentle soul, as beautiful inside as she was out. She was funny, she was warm and loving and playful . . . Honestly, she seemed too good to be true. As I drove her home after a very successful date, she asked me to come inside.

My gut dropped.

'In case you need to use the toilet . . .' she fumbled.

I thought it was so cute that she clearly wanted me to come inside but tried to cover it up by saying it was just in case I needed to wee.

We awkwardly danced around different topics of conversations, neither of us really knowing what the next move was going to be. After such a wonderful night together, I would have loved to have kissed her – respectfully of course. But again, this was new for me – making the moves with girls seemed so foreign. I was nervous to do anything that might make her uncomfortable, and (I found out after discussions much later) so was she.

Feminine-to-feminine dynamics are interesting when you initially start dating. It's not like there's a conversation – 'Just to clarify, you are gay, yeah?' – to confirm their interest in you. I spent a lot of the night stressing that perhaps she had accepted this dinner date as a friendly offer – just two gals going for a few wines and a hangout.

What if I go to kiss her and she freaks out?

I was stressing, panicking that I may have interpreted this catch-up totally wrong.

(We piss ourselves laughing about it now, how every sign was there for both of us to see yet neither of us was brave enough to read the play for what it was.)

She walked me downstairs to my car, where I admit, I waited for 30 minutes in case she asked me to come back. But in the back of my head, that perfectly nice, friendly text conversation I'd been having with the other woman before my date was bubbling away.

It seems I had two women on my mind after all.

Chapter 16

A few weeks later, I was interstate for a work event and a colleague suggested we go to dinner – me, them . . . and the woman who'd suddenly showed renewed (albeit unexpected) interest. There was no harm – I was freshly dating someone else, after all, and thoroughly enjoying getting to know her. My blonde bombshell was a dream; she was everything I could have ever wished for in a girlfriend. She knew all about what had happened with this other woman; knew she'd strung me along for months and then left me heartbroken. She also knew we were having dinner together that night – honesty has always been a defining point of my relationships.

There was the faintest twist in my stomach as the three of us sat down at our table. I half expected her not to even acknowledge me after the way she'd acted the last time we'd been face-to-face . . . but this wasn't the woman who'd rejected me in the middle of a crowded pub. This woman was suddenly nice, she was warm and fun, and there was no trace of that stone-cold stranger I'd last seen. The girl that I'd Face-Timed every night for months was finally here.

The night wore on and my other friend left, off to catch a redeye flight back to Melbourne. We had a few drinks . . . and a few more, and the woman I'd once wanted so badly completely reappeared.

Trying to ignore what I felt deep down was happening, I was caught off-guard when she seemed to look deep into my soul. She was ready, she told me, if I was. Ready to be together.

I actually said no at first, hoping to protect my heart from being hurt again. Yet, a few more wines later, we booked a hotel room in the city and we were soon in bed together, having the sex I'd once longed for. But I felt nothing. No part of me wanted more after that night.

While Blondie and I had been dating, it wasn't 'official' yet − technically, I was still single, and I had every right to do what I did. Whilst this might not be what some would consider 'morally correct', I wasn't exclusive with anyone at that stage, and I went home happily the next day without a thought for the woman I'd just slept with. The sweet girl I'd been seeing for the past month deserved every chance, and I wanted to try to make things work with her.

But there was something else hanging over me: while the other woman had only returned to Australia from overseas recently, she was going to be heading off again in the next six months, with no indication of how long she'd be gone. Clubs from countries all over the world were trying to sign her and every part of me knew that this was my only chance to spend time with her. I was torn between trying to do the right thing by this beautiful basketballer I'd developed a genuine relationship with, but also following my heart back interstate.

By the end of December, I'd made up my mind.

Just a few days out from Christmas , the other woman had told me in a text that she loved me – and that did it. I knew it must have been a big deal for her to make that statement, and I couldn't help but respect her for doing what I felt she was doing – letting me in.

But how the fuck was I going to explain this to Blondie, who was now my girlfriend? Who I'd told only a week earlier was the one for me? I hadn't gone into this intending to hurt anyone, but I felt like I needed to see where this other connection could go. Did Blondie With The Bun deserve this? Not at all. But if nothing else, I was determined to always be 100 per cent honest with her, and I had to stand by that and do what was right for me. After coming so far in recent years, I'd learnt that I needed to listen to my intuition when it spoke up. She was wonderful, yes, but I'd only known her a month; I didn't owe her anything, I reasoned with myself.

After coming out of a ten-year relationship not all that long ago, I knew I deserved to explore life a bit; to take a risk, to make a mistake, to learn some lessons the hard way. I needed to do all of that.

Blondie and I were lying in bed. We'd just had sex and I rolled over to grab my phone when it buzzed on the bedside table. 'I love you, babe,' read the text. 'Please just come to me.'

Ooft. This was it.

I rolled back to face the girl I'd been with for over a month, the girl I'd just slept with.

'I've got to go,' I said, bursting into tears. 'I'm so sorry. There is no easy way for me to do this to you. And nothing I can say right now is going to make any of this better, but . . . I'm going.'

She lost her absolute mind at me – rightly so, given my disgusting behaviour – and stormed out of her house.

Shit! How can I get out of here before she comes back?

I was a complete fucking coward. I knew it at that moment, but I couldn't think of anything that was going to make this any easier for her as I had made up my mind. I grabbed all my stuff, snatched up my bag and scribbled out a short note for when she returned.

'I'm sorry.'

I ordered an Uber to take me to the airport there and then. There was no waiting – this was happening now.

The phone rang. I didn't want to answer, I didn't want to face the horrible thing I'd just done. She wanted to talk but it was too late, it was already done. My love in another state had already sent through confirmation of my flight directly to my email – there was no going back now.

'I'm sorry. There's no easy way to do this, I can't let you down slowly,' I told her. 'I'm going to her. I love her. And I am sorry . . . That's all I have to say,' I finished, the ice in my voice shocking me. I could barely believe I'd just done such an awful act to this woman who'd shown me nothing but warmth, sweetness and love from the moment we met.

But I knew where my heart lay.

As the plane landed, I sent a message to the girl waiting for me interstate.

Her reply came in an instant.

'Baby . . . I've got you. I love you.'

Three days later, it was over again.

Three days.

After I'd just mercilessly dumped someone who did not deserve to be treated badly; after I'd left my kids with their dad with no notice; after I'd sacrificed a lot of good things in my life to follow my heart and race to be by her side . . . I had hoped for more than this.

But she didn't want any pressure, she told me.

'I just can't do this,' she had said as I sat crying on her floor.

I wanted to scream.

I had been supposed to stay with her until Christmas Eve, but I went home a day early. When I'd left Melbourne, I had told my friends and my family, that I loved her, that I was 'going to get my girl'. Seventy-two hours later, I was sitting on a plane, sobbing all the way back home. Again.

I don't blame her for my actions in the lead-up to that moment – they were the choices I had willingly made. But I couldn't help thinking that if she had just not contacted me again, none of this would've happened.

Chapter 17

Ding!

    I was up early on Christmas morning – pretty normal when you have two kids bursting with excitement to see what Santa's left for them – so when my phone buzzed, I was already sitting on the lounge with it in my hand, taking pics of the present opening.

'Can I come see you? I want to talk.'

I ignored the message. I didn't any more drama, no matter how much I loved this woman.

On Boxing Day, I woke up to an email telling me she'd booked a flight to Melbourne. (She'd sent an email because I'd blocked her number on Christmas Day.) She rocked up at my doorstep that afternoon and it was like nothing had ever happened. We spent the night together before she flew home the next morning, leaving me more confused than ever.

My brain was all over the place in the week that followed. My Melbourne girl, my basketballer, was in touch with me too, trying to get us back on track. And I was weak, despite knowing very well that she deserved neither the hurt I'd already caused her, nor what I knew I was capable of doing again.

Meanwhile, my girl interstate was still curious to know where my head was at.

'I'm coming down to spend New Year's with you,' she texted me on the morning of December 29, putting a quick end to plans I had with my friends. 'I'm booking another flight.'

I knew she already had New Year's plans – a long-standing tradition with her friends and one that she wouldn't miss for the world. But she had decided to spend the time with me instead.

She wanted me to choose her. And yet there was me, torn between two loves.

She spent New Year's Eve with me, Jaryd and the kids, and even my mum – and when she went home the next day, I went back with her.

Now, I love the singer Lewis Capaldi and she knew it, so when we saw he was playing the next night, she jumped straight onto her social media to try to find us tickets.

'We have to go,' she said, insisting that she would pay anything to get to the show. And she did – because she knew how much I loved his music, how much it resonated with me, and what it would mean to me to see him live in concert. Her generous acts of kindness for those she cared about was a trait we shared – we both loved spoiling those around us.

And so we went – and had the most magical night together. Nobody knew we were dating at that point. There was speculation online but there was no hard evidence, and that night, we weren't two people living in the public eye. We were just us. We were in our own little magical bubble, just two more faces in the crowd, soaking in the live music and loving life in that moment together. Even though we were both public figures – me more so in Melbourne – it was a really beautiful time in my life. As someone who had openly lived so publicly online for so many years, sharing the ins and outs of her every move, I enjoyed being somewhere no-one knew me. Nobody even knew where I was, except for Jaryd obviously, as we were co-parenting. It was freeing to be anonymous, even if just for a few days. I could go visit her, slip in and slip out again without ever having to explain a thing.

We danced and drank white wine with our arms around each other that night, belting out Lewis Capaldi tunes while staring into each other's eyes and having the time of our lives. After the show, we went back to her apartment, which she shared with three others, and as soon as the front door closed, she pounced. It was 1am, and her flatmates were asleep upstairs, but she didn't care.

I've always been a sexual being, but this was next level. There was something so passionate and carefree in it.

It was the best night we ever had together as a couple and it was significant for our relationship, too. It was the first time I felt like we were finally getting our shit together after a few months of back and forth, of broken hearts.

The next few days together were perfect. She wanted to introduce me to her family, which I could tell was a big deal for her. As someone whose family is her top priority and her greatest pride – the people she respects unconditionally – this was huge. I met her parents, sister and her brother's wife and kids. They welcomed me into the fold with open arms, and just like I had with her, I felt instantly connected to them. It was as if I'd known them my whole life. I could see a future here, a future with these incredible people as my in-laws, this big, loving family, so full of laughter and kindness and so beautifully supportive of one another and of me. I spent a day on the beach with them, timing sprints between her and her big brother and holding her nervous niece's hand in the waves – and I felt like I'd again found my place.

She now appeared to be serious about me. But still, I needed some reassurance. We had already broken up twice – I needed to know it wasn't going to happen again. As magical as our time together had been, as much as we'd finally started to get into a groove, I felt we were living in limbo. I'd skipped out on real life to play house in this fantasy, but how were we going to make this work long-term? I have kids; I needed some sort of stability. I couldn't be a fly-in-fly-out fling.

I broached the subject the day I was due to head back to Melbourne, but didn't receive the answer I was hoping for.

I didn't need her to publicly announce that we were together; didn't ask her to start calling me her girlfriend. I just wanted to hear her say, 'Yes, now I am committed to you; you've got me', or something like that. But it was too much; it was too soon, she said, for that kind of pressure. She told me she wanted to take things slower.

As I rode to the airport to catch my flight home, I mentally called it. I had read the play here myself, and after everything I'd been through, I wasn't going to let this happen again.

We kept texting after I got back to Melbourne but hadn't made plans to see each other again. So, I was surprised when, a few days later, she told me she wanted to come to see me the following week.

'Look, I don't know. I just need a bit of time. I don't feel as if I'm able to get a straight answer about us, our relationship, so I just need to reflect on some things,' I told her.

'I love you! My walls are down now . . . I want to make this work . . .'

But I couldn't do it. I could see a pattern emerging. It wasn't that I didn't want to – I did, desperately – but I just needed some breathing space. For three weeks, I'd been swapping back and forth between two women – my two girl-friends, for all intents and purposes, who both knew about each other, but it still wasn't sitting right. I didn't feel safe in the position I was in and I needed to take some time for me. I called it. We were done.

Within a few weeks, I'd reconnected with the beautiful blonde in Melbourne, who'd patiently waited as I leapt between the two cities, loyal despite everything I'd put her through. While there seemed to be a ball and chain attached around my ankle elsewhere, I was handcuffed to Melbourne, too. We went to dinner, and it was the most beautiful feeling to be back in her calm, gentle presence. It didn't matter whether we labelled ourselves as a couple or not – I always knew where I stood with her and it was nice to feel that acceptance. It was respectful, it was easy. It was stable and comfortable and beautiful – and it was exactly what I needed after a dramatic few weeks.

~

When COVID-19 hit, a whole lot of unprecedented changes happened that no-one could've ever expected. One of these was an Olympic qualifier, a major sporting event. Having Olympic qualifier games in your own country is unheard of, so this was a major sporting event for the country – not to mention a huge moment for women's sport – and no matter who I was or wasn't dating, I had to be there.

My interstate girl *was* playing, though; and even though I would've gone regardless, I had to admit, the chance to see her play on home soil was irresistible. I'm an avid sports fan – I'd obviously dated (and married!) a sportsperson in the past, and I have always loved supporting my partners, but in the short time she and I had been together, I'd never had the chance to watch her play live – something we'd spent a lot of time discussing.

'I'd love to look up into the crowd and see you,' she had once told me. It replayed in my head over and over.

I had to get to that game.

I kept telling myself that I just wanted to be there for this momentous event in Australian women's sport, and was attending with other friends, but deep down I knew something would happen between us if I wasn't careful, so I put an insurance policy in place: I took my daughter with me.

I thought I was being so smart.

If Florence is with me, I can't go out for a drink after the game.

We'll go, it'll finish, and I'll take Florence back to our apartment and put her to bed and I'll go to sleep. And I'll fly home to Melbourne the very next morning.

That insurance policy didn't work out too well.

My manager knew everything that had happened between us in the past and he tried to warn me against going.

'Sophie, what are you doing?' he'd asked. 'You know you're putting yourself in a dangerous spot.'

'No, it'll be fine, I'm just taking Floss to see the soccer! It's fine.'

Who the fuck was I trying to kid?

I didn't go there with the intention of anything happening between us, I really didn't. But I'd be lying if I said that I didn't want to see her. It wasn't just the game, it was *her*. I didn't want to speak to her, I didn't want to interact with her at all. I just wanted her to know I was there supporting her. But when her family spotted me in the crowd and made a beeline for me during the game, I was completely shocked.

'Oh my God, Soph! Hi!' Her sister swept me into a tight hug – far from the reaction I expected to receive after recent events.

'Sophie! We've missed you,' added her mum, following closely behind.

I had purposely tried to stay away from these people, made sure I wouldn't be seated anywhere near them. This was her family – I had broken up with her. I had no right to insert myself into their dynamic, not that day, not ever. But they were insistent.

'Why are you sitting over here by yourself? Come and sit with us in the family section!'

They all knew perfectly well what had happened between us, but they were such beautiful, accepting, non-judgemental people. Their approach was, if she knows you're here and she's okay with it, we're okay with it too. They didn't ask questions; they didn't see it as any of their business.

'C'mon, Soph!'

I didn't want to be rude but . . . No, no. I couldn't sit with them. I *couldn't*.

I did.

The pride I felt as I sat there, surrounded by her family, watching as she played pounded in my chest. Her team was vying for a spot in the Games and she was in the thick of it, helping them take home the win. It was incredible. More than once during the match she looked up and I could've sworn she'd picked my face out in the crowd. I didn't know how that would even be possible and yet, at the same time, *of course* she did – because that was just us. It's how we were, magnetised, connected on some other level. We could never quit each other, no matter how hard we tried, because there was an invisible string drawing us together that could never be broken.

The game wrapped up and they were standing around taking photos. My back was to the field and Floss started bouncing around in my arms, waving.

'Mummy . . . LOOK!'

I turned around and it was her, hands on hips, staring up at me. My world froze as our eyes met. It sounds cliched, but when this woman looked at me, when she looked into my eyes, I melted. It didn't matter that we hadn't seen each other or even spoken in weeks. It didn't matter that the last words we'd said were said in anger. It didn't matter that I'd dumped her, taken up with someone else. In the instant she looked into my eyes, I was hers again.

This wasn't a one-off, it's how it had always been between us. With one look, my soul was hers. She would look deeper into me than anyone else ever had, ever could, and she had my heart.

'I hate you . . . but I'm so glad you're here,' her expression seemed to say, as she held my gaze for what felt like an eternity.

From that moment, I was gone. Game over. She jumped the fence and came up into the crowd – something she *never* did – and made her way to me.

'Hi . . . how are you going?'

Our first words in nearly two months.

'Good, good . . . great game.'

We chatted for a moment, nothing more than small talk, before she was whisked away for the obligatory post-match photos with family and fans, but she kept looking over, checking that I hadn't left.

She wants me here.

I didn't need to be by her side, it was enough for her to feel my presence, to know I was supporting her. But time was ticking on, and I had to get Florence to bed. I made my way over to say goodbye.

'Thanks for coming,' she said, leaning in to give me a hug. 'What are you doing now?'

'Nothing, just taking this one home, she needs to get to bed,' I replied, bouncing Florence on my waist.

'Cool well I've just got to have a shower, pack my bag, I could probably be there in about half an hour.'

It wasn't a request; it was a statement. It was presumptuous, so arrogant to assume that I'd allow it – and I fucking loved it. This unshakable confidence was one of the things I loved most about this woman and I found myself agreeing in spite of myself.

An hour later, Floss was fast asleep, and the woman was on my doorstep, a bottle of my favourite wine in hand. We talked for hours – we always had this uncanny ability to pick up where we left off, like nothing had ever happened. She always felt like home, and I don't know if that was a great thing or a terrible one, but it made it very easy to slip back into the feeling that we were girlfriends – and do so with very little guilt about the girl I was seeing back in Melbourne, who thought I was spending the night alone.

How could something that felt so right possibly be wrong?

I knew what I was doing was morally and ethically wrong. But I'd done commitment. I'd been married. I'd spent my entire twenties changing nappies. In this moment of my life, I was selfish because I felt like I *deserved* to be selfish.

So, when I sat up with this woman, drinking wine and talking until seven o'clock in the morning, there was no guilt, nothing weighing on my conscience, because in that moment, I was exactly where I needed to be.

Chapter 18

After the qualifiers in early 2020, my love life was finally in a good place. After months of anguish, the intense highs and lows were over and I'd come out the other side at last, with my love by my side. I'd called things off with the beautiful blonde in Melbourne once and for all – a relief after the agonising back-and-forth I'd been doing to her. I certainly hadn't taken any pleasure in hurting her over and over again.

Now my girlfriend, my interstate girl, invited me away on holiday with her family in early March. We were going to go to Fiji, something we were both so excited about, though COVID-19 forced us to change the destination. This invitation felt like a huge step, given how important her family are to her. She's travelled the world since she was sixteen, so hasn't always seen them much, and I could tell by the way she watched me interact with them that it made her happy.

'You really fit in here,' her brother told me, not having a clue how much that made my heart sing. 'Do you two ever talk about having kids?'

The question was unexpected. After all, we hadn't been together that long, in the scheme of things – but, yes, we had talked about it. More than once. I could see her mum as the grandmother to our babies, her sister as auntie to my kids. I saw her brother as my best man in our wedding – I could picture our life together so clearly.

'Yeah, we've talked about it,' I replied with a smile, keeping the name we'd already picked out to myself.

'I love that. That makes me really happy.'

Her brother is her idol, so that fact that he felt so comfortable asking about me having a serious future with his sister . . . for me it was a sign that we were meant to be. But I also know now that my ability to see our life planned out in such precise, beautiful detail scared the hell out of her.

With her approval, I shared photos of us together on my Instagram, ones her sister had taken of us together, knowing I would be revealing for the first time in a public forum that was dating a woman. She commented with love hearts on my posts, writing, 'Love you babe.' And so, just like that, I went public with not only our relationship but also, for the very first time, my sexuality. While there'd been speculation in the media for more than a year around my and Jaryd's split, it hadn't been confirmed – I hadn't ever 'come out' – so this was a monumental moment for me in terms of owning my newfound identity.

The media, of course, had a field day and it was all over the headlines: *Sophie Cachia Holidays With New Girlfriend!*

I hate to think what those stories must've done to my ex, who I'd been with only a few weeks earlier. But for the first time in what felt like forever, I was content and I was happy. I was in love and I was *loved*, too. I'd chosen to put myself first and while I hated the pain I'd caused along the way, I knew I'd done the right thing by myself.

A few days after that blissful week with her family, she was set to play a grand final in Melbourne. I couldn't have been more excited to see my girl on the field again, this time in my own hometown, but there was a bit of urgency to it, too. We both knew she could be called up to go back overseas at any moment, and it was likely coming in the next couple of weeks, so I didn't want to miss a single chance to spend time with her before that day came.

'I can't wait to come watch you!' I texted her a couple of nights ahead of the game.

'You don't have to come. Let's please not make a big deal of it,' was the reply I got, instantly sending my mood plummeting.

Why would I not go and watch her soccer grand final?

Why is she being weird about it?

Does she not want me there?

'What do you mean? Of course I'm going to be there,' I shot back.

It wasn't a big deal, she told me. It didn't matter. 'It's just a game.'

We bickered a bit but finally we agreed that, yes, I would be there. It was a great game, even though they lost, but she had to go straight back home after the game for a team function.

'I just want to say I'm really sorry,' she messaged me when her plane touched down. 'I was really stressed in the lead up to the game. I did want you there and I am so thankful for you. There's nothing I love more than knowing you're in the stands watching me. I am so proud of you, too. I love you so much, babe.'

Aww!

'Get off your phone darl, go and enjoy your night with your teammates,' I replied. 'Have fun, I'll chat to you tomorrow. Love you xx'

When she called at 11am the next day, I could tell something was up. She seemed distant, her words clipped and short, and she didn't seem to be engaging fully with the conversation. We spoke about her night – 'Yeah it was good, I had the best time . . .' – but I wanted to plan out our next moves. While the ongoing pandemic meant we didn't know exactly when she would be leaving to go back overseas, we knew it would be soon and I wanted to see her as much as I could before she left, but my top priority was organising my kids.

'I don't mean to throw this on you, but obviously I want to come up again and see you and your family before you go . . .'

'Oh, we don't need to decide that now,' she interrupted.

'I know but if you're leaving next weekend, I'm going to have to come sometime this week. Have you heard any more about it or . . .'

She cut me off again. 'We'll talk about it later.'

Ouch. Sorry that I want to see my girlfriend before she moves overseas . . . What the fuck?

'Well, I thought I might bring the kids up too, they love you and they'll want to say goodbye to you too.'

Silence.

'Um, I've got to go, I've got things to do. We'll talk later, okay?'

She hung up the phone, leaving me stunned and angry. What had just happened? Why was she acting so weird? I needed to know.

'That was a bit rude,' I banged out in a text message, frustrated that she'd apparently gone cold after telling me how much she loved me only the night before.

Her reply was the last thing I expected.

'Look, I can't do this anymore.'

What . . . the fuck is she talking about?

I was floored. Less than 24 hours prior, she'd said how much she loved me, appreciated me, wished she was in bed with me instead of going out with the girls. A few days earlier, we'd been holidaying with her family like we'd been together forever.

What the fuck had changed?

Was she freaking out because I suggested that I bring my kids – whose life she'd been in for nearly six months – up for a few days to farewell her?

I was completely dumfounded – until I found out that her departure to go overseas had been booked for the following week. She knew she was leaving, and I figured she must have wanted to cut it off before she was gone.

The morning after, the country went into lockdown for the first time. I was a fucking wreck – and I couldn't leave the house, couldn't see anybody. I was broken and distraught. This was the third time I'd let her back in, that I'd told my friends and family we're back together, that we were solid this time.

I'd been on holiday with her family only a week earlier. I could see our future – so to have her say that it wasn't working was heartbreaking.

There was also a bigger picture for me. It wasn't just another relationship breakup – she was supportive of me going public with not only us, but with my sexuality. It was in the newspapers; it was all over the fucking internet. The speculation over my sexuality and my split with Jaryd had been going on for a year and now I was finally in a position to feel safe enough to share some of that. Me posting a photo of us on social media affected my life far more than just, 'Hey, here's me with a new partner'. I'd announced this huge life change – not just to strangers, but to my family, my friends, my colleagues. I was coming out to the world . . . and three days later, the relationship in which I felt secure enough to make that move was no longer.

I was ashamed and deeply embarrassed.

As the weeks in lockdown dragged on, I was inconsolable. I learnt through mutual friends that her move had been put on hold indefinitely. The world had stopped, travel was off the cards for everyone, and there certainly wasn't any professional sport happening, so she was as stuck at home as I was in Melbourne. Except of course, for me, my world was collapsing around me for a million other reasons. Articles were still circulating online about us, and I was still getting emails from magazines and radio stations asking for interviews – not just with me but my 'girlfriend' too. They had no idea we'd broken up just days after I posted that happy snap. I was hysterical. I wasn't eating, I was hurting myself, and I was calling her constantly on FaceTime begging her to tell me why she didn't love me.

'Soph, people break up all the time,' came her response. 'You'll be fine.'

I wish I could say that this is where I was brave enough to cut the cord, where I stopped putting up with the uncertainty, where I finally picked myself up off the floor and came back, better than ever.

And I did try. I really did put up a good fight. She was trying to explain herself when her apologetic texts rolled in, but I refused to answer. She would call me, but I didn't pick up. I declined FaceTime and I ignored replies to my stories on Instagram. The state of my mental health insisted on it.

'I'm sorry for what I said, it came out wrong,' she would message me. 'I didn't actually mean that. I was just emotional.'

'Please, Soph, just talk to me.'

She called Jaryd asking for advice.

'You can't keep doing this . . . if you're coming back this time, you are coming back for good.'

'Yes,' she'd apparently said to him. 'I love her.'

That might've been what broke me. I could sense real remorse in her messages, and I could see how hard she was trying to get me back, the lengths she was going to, the effort she was putting in. Even someone from her family network reached out to me, asking me to give her another chance, to simply hear her out

She was a mess, they said. They'd never seen her like that before.

I'd been so strong, held out for so long. A part of me knew that if I caved, I'd end up back in her arms and then probably regret it. But I had so much respect for the person from her side who'd reached out, I didn't want to ignore that plea for help.

'I will respond to you, but I have a lot of things to say. So just let me do it in my own way,' I typed out in a text, hitting send.

'Thank you, that's all I needed,' came her instant response. 'I just needed acknowledgement.'

Doing it 'my own way' turned out to be writing a seven-page long email listing my concerns and feelings, asking all the questions I'd felt had gone unanswered in our breakup.

The next time she called, I didn't ignore it and we ended up speaking on the phone for six hours. She opened up to me about the challenges she'd been facing, how her world had changed in lockdown . . . She'd realised how much she valued my support.

The country was still in lockdown at this stage, but she joked that she might come down to stay with me for a little while and we had a bit of a laugh about it.

Two days later, she'd packed her car, driven to Melbourne and moved in with me and my children.

Chapter 19

As much as I might criticise her, I had been putting somebody else in a very similar position at the same time. It was such a brutally confusing time for me, experiencing the turmoil of those emotions yet simultaneously doing the *exact* same thing to someone else. It wasn't in my nature – I'd spent my entire life an empath and overly compassionate but somewhere along the line, I had become okay with what I was doing.

You see, at the same time, I'd been back in contact with my blondie – the one I'd left *again* only weeks earlier.

We weren't back together, but we had reconnected, we were hanging out a bit, talking on and off here and there. But when the break-up-make-up cycle kicked off for the millionth time with my interstate girl, I put a stopper in it. I just couldn't deal with having this amazing girl in my life, who I knew loved me – who had proven time and time again she'd show up for me – while I was navigating what was going on in another part of my life.

So, I called off yet another brief reunion before it got serious, in order to attempt to 'figure my shit out' for what felt like the 500th time. I didn't outright say that it was because the other woman was back, because technically, she wasn't. I explained that now wasn't a good time for us to reconnect; I needed to step away before it became serious, before I risked causing even again more hurt – even though I still managed to inadvertently do exactly that.

While at times it probably appeared that I was treating her badly, I believed I was doing the best I could with the situation I had found myself in. I spent a lot of time trying to forgive myself for being in love with two people at once. Yes, it was highly complicated, each of them offering different levels of compassion, desire and fulfilment for me. The reasons I loved them were polar opposite, too.

Feelings don't have an on-off button, though at times I'm sure we all wish they did. I was stuck in a place of loving someone who, looking back, I think didn't necessarily deserve that love at that time, and someone whose love I most certainly didn't deserve to receive.

Part of me did weigh up if it really was love for either of them or if it was infatuation with the uniqueness of the situation I was in with both of them. Going back to my theory and beliefs surrounding monogamy being a social construct, I was in favour of the notion of having love that overlapped for multiple people at once. And during this entire period of my life, I was never dishonest about where my feelings lay.

As someone who had always maintained full control in her relationships and who had lived a significant chunk of her adult life responsible for two children, I was deeply attracted to 'not having to take the lead' with one woman. She was just as sure of herself as I was, and it was hot. The confidence and the presence were inspiring. She was the type you'd compliment – tell her she looked good and she'd reply, 'I know.' She was 'the boss' and I loved not having to play that role. And I *loved* her playing that role for me. An entirely new relationship dynamic, it was refreshing, spontaneous and fun. Her certainty contrasted with her deep loving side, always taking moments when it was just us to look into my soul and tell me how grateful she was for me and for my support of her – and how much she did really love me. She was financially set, too, not that I needed her money – I earnt double and then some myself. And I certainly didn't need her profile or notoriety. But the way she could 'look after' me was something I hadn't encountered for a while. There was a real 50-50 balance in the life load – someone who was equally as generous and who spoilt me, just as I had done for those I love for so long. It was nice to feel 'comfortable' in that sense, to not have to always be the one worrying about making the money. She was always leading the charge with dinner bookings, making plans for us, holding my hand, walking out in front as we moved through a crowd. But being comfortable being openly 'gay' was super-reassuring, too. I could finally be exactly who I wanted to be with her – and she was so proud of me in everything I did.

But it was the chase for me, too. She was my drug and I was addicted to her. Though I knew at times it wasn't healthy, I was addicted to the highest of highs I found in her – though I ignored the come-down lows.

The other woman was, on paper, everything I thought I'd want. A true empath like myself, who provided me with nurturing and care that always made me feel safe and accepted, even at my absolute worse. The one you could sit in an empty room with for hours, deep in conversation, and never once get bored. The simplest things in life were fun just because I was with her. She's the one that 'everyone liked' because her positivity was infectious. She would bring joy to anyone she was around and fill the room with an energy that has to be witnessed to be understood. Hilarious doesn't even begin to describe her. How someone so sexy could be equally as goofy and down-to-earth, I didn't know. My family absolutely adored her, and she always left a significant impression on my children who asked about her every day, even when we weren't in contact – something I could never ignore. She was the one who constantly made me feel appreciated, and who was a deep romantic just like I was – setting up cooking nights or home spa retreats was a regular for us, because the thing we loved most was simply being in each other's company. Our sexual natures were so aligned and she always made me feel comfortable to express and explore my desires. And she satisfied me – more than anyone else ever had.

She hadn't always had the easiest of rides throughout her life, but she wasn't bitter or hard on the surface – she was understanding, always considerate and she was my calmness. And for all of these reasons, I feared her. Because she was so damn perfect. The perfect future, the perfect wife, the perfect mother . . . for someone who just needed to be set free for a while.

~

It might sound like it was easy for me, flipping back and forth between these two women I loved, but in reality, it was destroying my mental health. I wouldn't wish it on anyone, to be in this position, not only hurting someone you care about, but also yourself, over and over. There was a constant internal battle raging inside me. For a while, sure, I knew I was being selfish, and I was okay with that. I am not playing the victim because I willingly put myself in that position, time and time again. Having just come out of a nearly a decade-long relationship, I really believe I deserved to have some fun, to enjoy my freedom, and to experience life a little. But it became obvious pretty fast that I had real feelings for both of these women. I loved two people and I loved them for totally different reasons, each giving me something the other didn't.

I had someone who I had loved from the first photo of her I saw on Instagram, that big, gorgeous smile and the piercing eyes I'd been known to melt for. One who I'd bonded with from our very first FaceTime call from opposite sides of the world – yet I felt like we just couldn't ever quite make it work. And then I had this other woman – too good to be true – who I knew could give me a happy, fulfilling life . . . but I just didn't know if I wanted what she had to offer. She was so pure, so nice and I was petrified to hurt her as well; terrified of making a commitment to another 'nice' person . . . would I run again? I'd made a commitment to my 'nice' husband and that hadn't worked out – what if it happened a second time?

Yet here I was again, allowing a person back into my life, into my home, despite the hurt I'd experienced.

The plan was for my interstate girl to come down and simply *be* with me. We'd get through this frightening, uncertain time in the world time together. She'd help with the kids, we'd train together, and I really thought it would be good for me to have someone else there with me. We had no idea if or when she'd be travelling again, whether going overseas was off the cards for good or just a little while . . . just like the rest of the world, we had no idea what was coming next. So we bunkered down together and played happy families.

And it was beautiful . . . But it was exhausting. We had so much fun together; it was fiery, passionate and we complemented each other perfectly. But we also fought – oh my God, the fights. We had always brought out the best and the worst in each other but put us in the same house for five weeks and at times we were explosive. The whole relationship was one of extremes. The highs sent me soaring, but the lows left me in ruins. I can't and never will only blame her, either – we both contributed to that pattern. In moments, it mirrored my relationship with my own mother. I kept waiting for something to change, for her to love me in the way I wanted her to love me. With the obsessive, dependent love I gave her, I struggled to accept her for what she was – different to me and all I'd ever known. I can now understand the pressure that must have created. In some ways we were a match made in absolute heaven, two caring, loving, independent, career-driven women, complementing each other through life. But at a deep, fundamental level, we were also the worst pairing possible. We were two alpha females, a combination bound to end in tears.

My friends and family constantly asked me why I kept going back to her, even though our breakups left me so hurt. But this was exactly it, I realised – there was something about the rush of emotions, whether they were good or bad, that I found so appealing.

It felt like whatever she wanted to do, we did. Whatever she said, I agreed. If she wanted to nap? We napped. If she had had enough of me and wanted to sit on her own upstairs, I'd sit in the loungeroom waiting until she was ready for my presence again. None of this was through force or coercion, ever – I was simply happy to be her willing puppy dog.

I remember telling a friend once that I idolised her.

'That's not a good thing, Sophie,' he'd said. 'You've put her up on this pedestal. Now you're losing yourself.'

But I'd make excuses. I insisted that I liked this new dynamic – and I did, I truly did. I liked not having to make all the decisions; I liked not having to shoulder the financial pressure; I liked having this really independent person who was a boss in her own right, someone who really had her shit together. I couldn't see at the time just how much of myself I put aside to be in this relationship.

'I'll change to be who she wants,' I would tell myself.

During our time living in lockdown together – our longest stint of dating without breaking up – I had *completely* changed. I was no longer Sophie. I compromised on everything I held dear, on the things I would and wouldn't stand for in life. What's worse, I convinced myself that I needed to be this new, dulled-down version of myself in order for her to stay, so that she would keep loving me. In situations where I'd normally question what someone was saying, I held back. In the moments I wanted to jump and scream with excitement, I fixed my face into cool composure while fist pumping inside so as not to be embarrassing.

In the end, I spent so much time trying to be something I wasn't that I had no idea who I was anymore. I knew I wasn't me – far from it – but I loved her, and she loved me too. And that was all I cared about.

~

I never thought I'd say it, but after five weeks of us living together in lockdown, I was so happy when she left. I just wanted my space back . . . but not a week later, I was on my way up to see her again. We travelled back and forth like that for the next few weeks, always driving nine hours each way because air travel was still on hold. I was getting trolled mercilessly online – 'Oh look, she's taken off on her kids again' – but anyone who's a mum knows that leaving your kids for a week, ten days at a time isn't an easy thing to do, even with several FaceTime calls a day. I'm not sure if she appreciated the toll it took on me, being so far away from my children. But again, I unfairly expected her to understand, despite motherhood being something she hadn't personally experienced.

She was dealing with her own shit, too. With the halt on sport and travel, her career was up in the air like never before – but as a world-class athlete, she still had offers coming in from overseas teams . . . God, I was so proud of her. But I also knew it meant that she could up and leave at the drop of a hat, jetting off to a new life in Paris, London or anywhere else in the world.

It wasn't an easy time for her, but I cherished playing that role of emotional supporter, and she'd always express her gratitude to me for being there for her. I was there for the tears, for the hard conversations, the arguments and the stress. I was there by her side when at times contracts were uncertain. It was always me. I was on that roller-coaster with her: when she felt a low, I felt a low; when she had a win, I had a win. I wanted to be her peace during a very emotionally fraught time.

She was close to signing on to play soccer with a team overseas, and when her contract was announced, I felt she had already started to distance herself from me. I suppose might've been doing it knowing that she was about to move – maybe hoping to make things easier on herself, on me, when she did eventually go.

We hadn't overly discussed what would happen when she left – which was probably to our detriment. It was a lot to process for both of us . . . so we didn't. We stayed in our love bubble, mostly ignoring the inevitable. Sure, we discussed a few different scenarios, a few ways we might work the situation, but we never came to any kind of decision regarding us or made any plans. But how could we? With COVID-19 having only been around for a few months at that stage, we didn't know yet exactly how the world was going to change. Would things be back to normal by Christmas? Would we be five years on, still not allowed to travel internationally? She didn't like to make decisions without all the information, so I knew not to push that on her, even though it was killing me not to have any clarity about the future.

At the same time, I didn't know if I wanted to commit to a long-distance relationship with someone I might not see for another two years, either. I knew that I loved her unconditionally and that the thought of losing her was a living nightmare. I couldn't fathom a life without her, even if that could only be speaking on the phone from opposite sides of the world. It's how our relationship had started – could I do it again, possibly for years this time?

All I knew was that I felt stuck in Australia. I felt imprisoned in my own life. I had my two kids and I couldn't leave. At that point, I would've given anything to be able to pack my bags and move with her that instant, but that just wasn't ever going to be an option – and life circumstance was a difficult pill to swallow.

I feel ashamed admitting this, but for the first time in my life, I regretted having my children, and I really struggled to come to terms with that feeling, too. I love my kids so much and I wouldn't give them up for the world, but I was experiencing this bitterness towards the life I had signed up for and it was a real shock to the system.

If I didn't have kids, I could be travelling with the love of my life right now.

If only I didn't have my kids, I could follow her everywhere.

If I didn't have my kids, we could be together.

Those dark thoughts were so invasive, and they plagued me. I felt like a horrible person and a terrible mother. It wasn't my kids' fault I was in this position, but it was the first time as a mum, as a woman, that I felt any kind of regret for the way my life had panned out.

While I was facing my internal struggles, she seemed to be doing fine. That's how it appeared to me. I suppose, as a professional athlete, she'd grown used to saying goodbye to family and friends, to having teammates who are best friends one season, and then living in a different country the next, and I wondered if living that way for so long had desensitised her to those kinds of farewells. But it killed me further to witness how okay she outwardly seemed with the fact that this – us – could all be coming to a crashing halt.

Even in our final days together, she didn't seem fazed. I'd flown interstate, knowing the state borders would be closing soon and that it would be our last chance to see each other before she left Australia. We went to the beach for a few days, and it was very emotional for me because I knew this could well be the last time – maybe ever – we would have dinner at our favourite restaurant, lie in bed together as we listened to the waves crash on the sand, share avocado toast at our favourite little cafe. I wasn't crying the whole time, but it really hit me on our last day. We'd said goodbye to each other so many times, but we always knew we'd see each other in a week, two weeks. There was always the next meetup to look forward to.

How do you say goodbye forever?

How do you let go of someone when you don't want to?

And I wasn't just saying goodbye to someone I loved. I was also saying goodbye to a future I saw for us together; a future I so desperately wanted, with absolutely no certainty around whether it would ever come to pass. We'd picked out our children's names, we'd talked about marriage, how we would own houses in both cities. She was going to pick out our couch because she didn't like my colourful furniture choices . . . And when she retired, we'd settle down together in Melbourne.

I didn't live in a fantasy land. We knew the next few years would be challenging, but we'd had those conversations; I wasn't making it all up. I'm sure she had, at that point in time, envisaged life in the future with me.

It was so difficult for me to finally have to face the truth of her leaving, even though I always knew it was coming.

To me, she always seemed so composed, when all I wanted to do was sob uncontrollably.

I couldn't handle her being gone and I loved her too much to hide that.

~

I admit, she did let some emotion slip through a couple of times the day I left for Melbourne – our last day together. We were sitting on the beach, devouring our last meal of fish and chips, watching the tide roll in because I had to go to the airport to fly home.

'I have something for you,' I smiled cheekily, reaching into my bag. On a whim, I'd gone shopping that morning to buy a piece of jewellery I knew she'd been lusting after for a long time. She'd always said she'd buy it for herself one day, for a special occasion, and I often wondered why she hadn't. She certainly had the money to get it – she had a love of designer shoes and bags, just like me. We'd always bonded over our love of high-end brands and loved giving each other extravagant gifts. I knew that, since this would be the last time I saw her for who knows how long – maybe forever – I was going to get it for her.

I passed over the bag and she pulled out the box, the brand's signature packaging a dead giveaway for sure. But when she opened it, I could tell she wasn't expecting to see what was sitting there, nestled into the velvety fabric. The look on her face was one of absolute shock. Slowly, she lifted her eyes to meet mine and burst into tears.

I'd rarely seen her cry – but now she was bawling inconsolably, hugging me, shaking as she put it on.

Oh my God, she loves it so much!

'Soph, it's absolutely perfect,' she said, shaking her head, tears streaming down her face. I'd never seen her cry like that before. It seemed to go deeper than sadness, though at the time I couldn't put my finger on the other emotions that were tangled up in that moment for her.

We packed up our things and made our way to the airport, a solemn mood settling over us. This was it. The border would be closing the next day and wouldn't open again before she left. It was our final goodbye.

As we hugged, I was absolutely hysterical. I didn't know what to say. It's not every day that you say goodbye – possibly forever – to someone that you are so in love with. We kissed and we hugged, holding each other for dear life.

'I know it wasn't always easy,' I choked through my tears, 'but for me, it was always worth it.'

Her face cracked, tears rolling down her cheeks, her silent sobs in sharp contrast to my breathy cries.

We hugged.

We both turned around.

And we walked away.

Chapter 20

I've had a tenuous hold on my mental health for a long time and I've ridden the waves since adolescence – an unhealthy see-saw between thinking I'm magically cured and wondering if I'll be 'crazy forever'. I recall when I first discovered the release that cutting myself seemed to offer: when emotional pain was unbearable, physical pain would somehow ease it, pulling the focus away from the tearing feeling in my chest, the reverberating noise inside my mind.

I was thirteen or fourteen when I first took to my own skin with a pair of scissors. I played netball with a girl who would often come to training with large cuts all down her arm. We all knew what they were, but the taboo of mental health back in early 2000s meant that no one ever asked her about it or checked in to see if she was okay.

Obviously, *she wasn't.*

I didn't believe myself to be depressed back then, but I was so intrigued by what she'd done that I went home one day and tried it. A pair of scissors pulled from my school pencil case was all it took for me to become addicted to the physical pain I felt when adding fine cuts to my body.

It didn't have to be my arms. Down my thumb was a common choice, and into my thighs, too. I self-harmed very sporadically throughout my teenage years, a couple of times a year, perhaps, when my train of thought took me to darker depths – a place of no return.

I can't comment from personal experience, but I imagine the way I feel about it now is not dissimilar to the way a reformed drug addict might feel. You don't want to be that person anymore; you know it's unhealthy and that it's not the life you want to live moving forward . . . but you'll never, ever forget how good it felt.

My older sister suffered from severe mental health issues as a child and teenager, too – there was always something happening with her. She rode an emotional roller-coaster of such extreme highs and lows, and while I certainly suffered from my own demons, hers was a path I never wanted to tread.

I did try to talk to my mum about how I was feeling a few times when I was younger – though I rarely felt heard.

I think she probably thought I was just copying my sister for attention or in an attempt to get the validation she seemed to be getting, but I could tell very early in life that these intrusive thoughts that made their way into my brain, eradicating all logic, weren't the norm. I knew that I would benefit from some professional help.

At the age of fourteen, I built up the courage to tell my mum one night in the kitchen that I wanted to see a psychologist. Knowing that my parents got my sister the help she needed, taking her to appointments and funding her treatment, I did expect I'd be shown the same support. It wasn't the case, though. I was questioned, told I was fine . . .

'What for?' she'd responded when I sought help. 'There's nothing wrong with you.'

These kinds of phrases instantly make a person with any mental health issues back down, sending them – sending me – into a shame spiral. But I didn't want to give up. I've always been tenacious like that. It had been the theme of my life so far, and it was no different when it came to my mental health: I had to be the one to take care of myself. So, I began dog walking and working casually at a hairdresser, doing small cash-in-hand jobs and saving up my $100 every fortnight for my psychology sessions, but eventually, I no longer could afford to go.

Jaryd was always so wonderful with my mental health. He still is. He has an inherently calming nature and even when he doesn't understand how I'm feeling, he has the emotional maturity to simply listen. To sit, be and listen without judgment. I found that such a wonderful trait in a young man.

As I've evolved and grown into an adult, and experienced being with various different partners, I've come to realise that everyone has their own mental health issues – some more severe than others and some more easily recognisable than others, too. While some think of mental health as only depression and anxiety, my own relationship experiences have shown me that mental health struggles can present in various different ways, from not being able to sleep to having difficulty with anger management, irrational decision-making, a lack of empathy, exacerbating turbulent situations, seeming to have various personalities, deep-seated insecurities, living in denial, narcissistic behaviours . . . These are just a handful I've seen in my own relationships.

I've also learnt that, while I've always been deeply aware of my own psychological issues, not everyone is privy to what's going on for them internally. Some people are so self-aware and others are in complete denial. Being on the self-aware side, I know when things are getting bad for me, when my mental health is beginning to crumble – and it didn't take long for it to spiral out of control after my girlfriend and I said our final goodbye at the airport.

She didn't leave for overseas straight away. We'd parted ways in early July and she was still here until the end of

August, early September, but the shift in our relationship was instant. It was the last time we were physically going to see each other, because the border closed the next day, and she would definitely be leaving the country before it opened back up. In hindsight, I think it was a simultaneously good and bad thing, because there would've still been a lot of back and forth if that decision hadn't been made for us.

We were still texting here and there, but there seemed to be a change in the tone of her messages that made it clear to me that our romance was done. I felt she was quickly stepping away, bit by bit, and I didn't want that to happen. Yet, I couldn't bear the thought of being ghosted completely.

I spent a lot of that time pretending I was okay with the situation when I really wasn't. My mental health was deteriorating as I tried to make out like I was happy, like I was thriving, going about my life without her in it. I desperately wanted to text her, to find out how she was feeling, if she'd heard yet when she'd be leaving. But she would have seen that as me smothering her, it would've been 'too much'. So, I left it. Our messages changed from 'Hey, babe' to 'Hi Sophie', an apparent coldness seeping into every word.

Whilst I was proud of her and her accomplishments, my good heart was further shattered by the fact I couldn't be there for her wins after we broke up. Time and time again I had been there when she needed me. I'd been there by her side for the many ups and downs leading up to getting her contract, always her number-one sounding board, but when it finally came time to celebrate, I wasn't a part of that. The night her contract was announced publicly, I received a message from her mum.

'We really wish you were here celebrating with us!'

I poured myself a glass at home and I sent a picture back.

'Me too. I bet you're all so excited.'

It was a beautiful moment, to be recognised and included by her mum, but it was the painful last nail in my coffin. I had her mum thanking me, saying she and the family wished I was there with them, but I didn't hear anything from her about it.

Credit to her, she stuck to her word and still assisted me with a media project I had planned months earlier – a short series of interviews with high-profile people to share on my social media. We filmed this episode having not spoken a word to each other in weeks, only communicating via my assistant on email. That day was painful and whilst my professionalism allowed me to hide my racing, broken heart during filming, I was still proud of her in that moment – and I admit, I got a little pleasure when she seemed to nervously fumble her way through some of her answers. But at that time, I was lying about how I was going, and it wasn't all because I didn't want her to know how I was feeling.

It was because it hurt more to imagine that she didn't care.

~

By the time September rolled around and she left the country, we weren't speaking at all. Weirder still, everyone thought we were still together – people assume we ended things when she left Australia, but it was over much, much sooner, when we'd said that final goodbye at the airport.

I had an epiphany some weeks later when it occurred to me that those tears she'd shed when I'd given her that gift on our last day together may not have been a mirror of my own devastation, but something else. Of course, she may've been genuinely sad over the course of events, but the look I'd seen in her eyes as her gaze drifted back and forth between me and the jewellery box – that emotion I couldn't name at the time – in hindsight, I now believe it was guilt.

She had known in that moment that we wouldn't speak again, I think. I truly believe she was crying because she felt so bad about what was about to unfold.

So now I was alone, in lockdown, nursing a broken heart, and I was in a really dark place. I was a vision of depression. I would sit for hours on end outside in my courtyard, grossly smoking cigarettes until 3am, staring at my washing that had been hanging on the line for two weeks, untouched. I didn't have the capacity to bring it in. I didn't want to go to bed because it would mean I'd just have to wake up and do it all over again the next day. We were in the middle of this horrific COVID-19 lockdown, there was nothing to do, and I was completely lifeless. I missed her, yes, but I also felt so completely abandoned. I wasn't suicidal because I felt like I was dead already.

I didn't need her to tell me that she loved me. I didn't need her to tell me that'd we'd figure things out, that we'd get back together. I just needed to feel as though she cared about me, as a human, as someone she'd once loved. I wanted her to ask if I was okay; to show that she cared about my wellbeing.

That's all I wanted.

What was happening in Melbourne at the time definitely played into my emotions, too. Our whole world was fucked. Unless you were in Melbourne at that stage, you can't understand, and maybe that was part of it — she had no idea how bad that time was, no understanding of how much I would be suffering, imprisoned in my home for so long — living as a single mother day in, day out, with no face-to-face connection with anyone else. Trying to do the very best I could for my children whilst drowning deeply in the emotional abyss.

I suppose I shouldn't have expected her to be able to hold me through that time — not just because we weren't together, but also because I don't think she ever knew quite how to help me. She always valued my nurturing skills — how I'd cook for her, taking into consideration her dietary requirements as an athlete (the menu usually consisted of salmon and crispy potatoes). Even the way I'd offer to make phone calls for her if she was feeling nervous. But she told me right from the get-go that the way I was so open with my emotions scared her and she didn't know how to handle them.

Being confident to share and show my feelings no matter what they are – love and happiness, disappointment and sadness, anger and fear – is a quality of mine that I've always owned. I never shy away from discussing how I feel, even if I know it's not going to be looked upon favourably. It's how I live my truth and I wouldn't be me if I didn't do it. It's part of my personality that I know is polarising to some, but admired by many, too.

Speaking your truth often comes with negative connotations – people think you're a loudmouth or argumentative, obnoxious and stubborn, but that's never been my view. I've always preferred to be brave enough to be disliked for who I was than to be liked for a watered-down version of myself just to blend into a comfortable crowd. Having deep and meaningful conversations that allow space for more than one perspective is something that fuels me. One of my favourite things to do is sit around with a few gins and discuss . . . anything! To learn the different ways people think and delve into their personal insights. For me, there's nothing more respectful than when you can say to someone, 'While I don't agree with that view, I find it really interesting that you think that way.' I find it quite humorous that we now live in a generation that has come so far in accepting people's unique and individual looks and lifestyles, but there's still so much contention surrounding the fact that our minds work so differently.

That was always an issue we faced.

Suppressing my emotions, needing to be heard and acknowledged, and not having that need met definitely played into my mental state as the days ticked by and I remained alone. I wanted to speak to her, but I was too scared to rattle her, to make her anxious, so I kept it bottled up. But I was dying inside. I didn't want to move on, and if that made me weak, fine – but I wouldn't dare admit it.

Is this what true heartbreak feels like?

I once thought I knew, but this onslaught of emotions was new for me.

Meanwhile, my 30th birthday was creeping ever closer. Never mind that I was heading into a new decade, a new life stage, in lockdown – I was also coming to grips with the stark difference between what I thought my life would be at 30 and the reality of what it was.

You've got your kids, you've got a good life. You should be happy.

But I was getting divorced. My girlfriend, the love of my life, had left. She was gone and I didn't know if I was going to see her again . . .

But it's your birthday, you're turning 30. You're meant to be happy.

My heart really wasn't in it, but nevertheless I planned an elaborate night with the kids to celebrate, where I dressed up as my favourite performer, Mariah Carey. Another thing COVID-19 had well and truly fucked for me was my 30th birthday celebrations. I had been planning on taking my whole family to the Greek Islands mid-year, and the week of my birthday, I was supposed to be in Las Vegas with my best friend, Taylah.

The truth of the situation was, I'd been struggling so much that Taylah had moved in with me a few weeks prior, and she was there with me on my birthday. We'd met a few years earlier at footy and at the time she was nineteen years old, and I was 27, so we were at very different stages of our lives, but somehow, we still hit it off immediately. Our personalities are so intrinsically similar; we just get each other, and she has been most loyal, supportive friend to me over the years I've known her. She's proven to me that age is no barrier to a genuine friendship. She's the type of friend who notices the little things, celebrates you as a person, shows up for you continually but is also okay to pull you up and question you when required. She would message me often to check in – 'Have you eaten today?' 'Have you had any water?' 'Let's go for a walk' . . . I don't think I've ever truly explained to her how important she was to me during that time. She was such an integral part of me getting through that period, helping me survive that stage of my life.

Taylah and I were sitting outside having a cocktail as the clocked ticked over to midnight. My birthday had officially begun.

Ding!

Taking a drag of my cigarette, I glanced at my phone, lit up on the floor beside me like a warning beacon.

It was *her.*

A perfectly timed message wishing me a happy day – but it was so much more than that.

She still cares about me.

After we'd had no contact for weeks on end, here she was.

She was overseas, in a completely different time zone, but had made the effort to wish me a happy birthday the minute it ticked over to midnight. I was so grateful, so appreciative, but it hurt my soul because all I wanted for my birthday was to be with her. We'd talked all year about my 30th, hoped and wished that we'd be in the same country for it. She'd spoken about what she'd get me, which winery she'd take me to, to celebrate. Despite the obstacles ahead of us, I always imagined she'd be by my side on my 30th.

Later that day, my favourite bunch of flowers from my favourite florist arrived. It was an arrangement she'd bought me before, when we'd been together, on more than one occasion. Previously, she said she hated buying and receiving flowers – they were a complete waste of money, she thought. But she knew how much I adored the gesture of fresh florals and she had learnt over time it was an act I cherished. She'd also sent me an expensive bottle of champagne – another sentimental gift, as it was one we'd often enjoyed on the couch together.

But it was the sentiment behind the bigger gift, which arrived later that day, that ripped my heart out and drove over it with a monster truck.

It wasn't the kind of present you get your ex, the girl you haven't spoken to in six weeks. It was the kind of gift you buy your girlfriend – something so personal, that speaks to who you are as a couple, as a unit.

I get packages all the time – deliveries, work, online shopping orders, whatever. But as soon as I saw this package sitting on my doorstep, noting its size, I intuitively knew exactly who it was from.

Gingerly, almost afraid of what I'd find, I peeled back the packing tape, opening the box to reveal a beautiful vintage record player – something I'd mentioned months ago that I wanted – and a Lewis Capaldi record. Instantly, I was transported back to that night we spent together at his concert at the start of the year, easily the best night of our entire relationship, our happiest time spent together.

A part of me died inside as I carefully lifted the vinyl out of the box. Half of my heart was singing – this was the most thoughtful present I could've ever imagined. But the other half was broken because I couldn't share it with her. You have to understand we hadn't been in ANY contact for weeks at this point. And whilst I believe her intentions were sincere, and she was genuinely trying to do something to make me happy, the sentimental gift was a double-edged sword and a painful reminder of what I no longer had.

I wanted to call her up, to ask why she would take me back to the best night of my life with her when she couldn't be there with me, and I couldn't be with her.

But I didn't call her. I simply sent a text. A very restrained, emotion-free text. I didn't want to scare her by telling her how I really felt.

'Thank you so much for your present, it was so beautiful,' I wrote. 'Looking forward to spending the night with my kids tonight.'

In my head, I added, 'I love you. I miss you. Why did you do this?'

'Hey, hope you've had a great day – you deserve it :)' came her reply.

I was left so awfully confused once again. She didn't seem to want to have anything to do with me . . . yet she'd gone to the effort of sending such a sentimental gift, one that showed she was still thinking about me. That present was *proof* I was on her mind.

No, no, no, no, no.

Was this true love? I don't think I'll ever know.

We were each other's potion and were constantly drunk on euphoria. But her love was always guided by rational thought and pure logic, while mine was driven by a belief in a romantic fairy-tale – hopeful that, through untold hardships, our souls' connection would always see us through.

I completely acknowledge my part and take responsibility for willingly returning to a situation over and over that perhaps I shouldn't have, stripping myself bare of any remaining self-worth each time. I can't and will not blame her entirely. And I will never disrespect the many good parts of our relationship. I was five years older than her, and my emotional maturity should have held me back on many occasions. I lived on edge the entire relationship, and I never relaxed into it or felt at ease.

Relationships can be like that, though. Just because a romance goes badly does not mean either party is a bad person – nor does it say anything about your worth or what you deserve.

Deep down, I know she is a beautiful person, but I continually ignored the red flags in our relationship. My heart still holds love and respect for her, however, because I truly believe she wasn't aware how deeply I had fallen. While it didn't make it any less painful at the time, I know she would never have caused me hurt or pain on purpose.

After my birthday, though, things only got worse.

Chapter 21

For the whole month of September 2020, I was taking part in a charity running event called Connor's Run, which raises money to help young people with brain cancer. I'd pledged to run 125km in the month, raising money for one of my best mates' nieces who had devastatingly lost her battle to brain cancer at just five years of age. On average, I needed to do about four or five kilometres a day to hit my goal, but some days – days when I needed more of an escape – I'd smash out more like 8km in a day, which was pretty huge considering I'd really never run in my life.

On the outside, I appeared strong, fit, and the people around me were telling me I looked incredible. They weren't wrong – my body had dramatically transformed since

I started running. But it was behind closed doors that the transformation really occurred. I'd never been unhealthier in my entire life. I was running publicly for charity and posting about it every day in order to raise funds, but what nobody saw was a frail, depressed woman who wasn't eating, who couldn't sleep for days on end; someone who was sitting and smoking cigarette after cigarette after cigarette before and after those daily runs.

I'd lost ten kilos in two weeks because I just couldn't eat. My anxiety was so rife, and had become so overwhelming, that I completely lost any feelings of hunger. Day in, day out, I was just drinking and smoking. Looking back, I don't know how my body survived that period of time. Everyone on the outside would tell me that I was thriving, not knowing I felt I was barely clinging to life.

The running itself was good for my mental health, even though every run I did, I was thinking about *her*. It was therapy for me – listening to music, my feet pounding on the concrete path, just trying to get through it, to make it to the end of each session. The pain I was feeling meant I went further – it was almost like I was punishing myself for being in this position. I felt like a fraud, running to fund research into kids' brain cancer, meanwhile I would immediately celebrate the end of every run with a cigarette. My skin was dull, my eyes hazy, my brain full of fog. I'd never been so unhappy.

I realised I was no longer experiencing heartbreak; I was experiencing grief, as if someone I loved had died, gone in an instant, never to return – and there was nothing I could do about it. The reality, of course, was that I was dealing with the metaphorical 'death' of someone who was still very much alive but was no longer in my life.

People were still asking me how she was going, if she was enjoying the new club.

'I have no idea,' I'd tell them, my voice devoid of any emotion.

'Wait, you guys don't even speak anymore?'

That question was a dagger to my heart. Every. Single. Time.

The issue wasn't that I was no longer her girlfriend. I hadn't known if I could commit to that. It was that fact that someone I loved so much, who I'd spent so much time with – close to a year by that stage, back and forth – and shared such huge emotions with seemed to be doing fine now that we were apart. In the past, we had always come back to each other, always. No matter what, we knew we had always loved each other. And now I was trying to accept this person being on the other side of the world and us maybe never seeing each other ever again.

Two weeks after my birthday, as I sat looking at the record player she'd sent, the extravagant bunch of flowers, now wilted – I should've thrown them away long ago – it all became too much.

I felt like I was going legitimately crazy. I *had* to reach out, had to know if she was struggling too. Just a quick message to check in . . . that couldn't hurt, right?

'I am missing you so much, but I hope you're well,' I typed.

Nothing. Nothing for two days, and when the reply came in, it felt as if it was from a stranger.

She simply thanked me for my message, told me she was well, hoped that I was, too.

Her response was calm and measured, and something snapped in me.

Is she fucking serious?

I let loose.

'What is *wrong* with you???' I typed furiously on my phone. 'How can you be okay? I am *struggling*. I am reaching out for help . . . you promised you'd always be there to support me. How can you do this to me?'

I didn't wait for a response before I sent another text.

'I am struggling. I MISS you and you're sending me some robotic answer . . . How you are so *fucking okay* with all of this?!'

The three little dots terrorised me as she composed a message back. The wait was agonising.

'I think it's best if you don't contact me again. Thanks.'

My heart dropped into my stomach and world around me spun. I called – no answer. I called again . . . straight to voicemail. She was declining my calls. I kept calling and calling, relentlessly trying to make her listen to me, to acknowledge my existence, screaming into the phone as I left her a voicemail.

I was out on a walk – the one hour I was allowed out of the house a day in lockdown – and people stared as I stalked along in a frenzy, shouting obscenities into the phone. I was set off and I was scared – unrestrainable, hallucinating, muscles trembling out of my control.

It was absolutely horrific.

I walked and walked until I felt like all the life had been sucked out of me. I sat on a park bench in the rain, completely numb to my surroundings, like a scene out of a movie. I recall taking a photo of myself in that moment of absolute rock bottom, not wanting to ever allow myself to forget how painful this moment felt.

What am I going to do?

Utterly defeated, I'd never been here before. It was a physical pain, this burning, searing hurt inside my chest, and I needed to release it somehow, to shift it from inside of me.

This is why people kill themselves. This feeling, right now.

I didn't think then that I wanted to take my own life. But in that moment, I could understand why someone would; how it might seem an appealing option, to simply not feel any pain anymore.

My logic had also been numbed by my emotional state and all I wanted was to ease my emotional torment. Somehow in the haze, I'd found my way back to my car. I climbed in, sat at the steering wheel and started the engine, the torrential rain pouring down around me in the now-dark night as I pulled out into the street.

By this point, I did want to die. I knew I didn't want to be here anymore.

But my babies, they don't deserve this.

In such an intense moment, I settled on the fact that I just wanted to feel pain somewhere other than my chest. I wanted to hurt myself badly on the outside, just so that I stopped feeling this agony inside of me.

The pain of breaking my leg – that will distract me from what I'm feeling.

It's raining, so it will seem like an accident. It's actually perfect . . .

I planned it all in my head as I drove around, looking for the right tree and trying to figure out how I could angle the car on the side so I would snap right through the bone – because, at least in that moment, I'd be in pain somewhere else. I just couldn't bear to hurt inside anymore.

The phone ringing interrupted my plans. I saw it was my manager, who'd been calling me constantly since this whole thing blew up. I'd been ignoring him.

Answer the phone now or you're going to do something stupid, Sophie.

That split second of logic, of rational thinking, was enough to snap me out of my blind mission to damage my body. I answered.

'Soph, where are you? Please drive home – it's going to be alright.'

SOPHIE CACHIA

I did what he asked and when I got there, I sat in my driveway, clinging to my phone, and poured my heart out for two hours. I told him everything. And he just listened. He heard me. It's no surprise to me that this man is now my best friend in the world – he has been there for me in a way that no-one else has and if he didn't call me in that moment, I don't know what would have happened to me. If he hadn't made himself available to simply be there for me, I might not be here today.

When I got inside, Jaryd was there with the kids. He stayed the night with me, as a family – I just couldn't be there alone, without a friend. After Floss and Bobby had gone to sleep, Jaryd came back into the living room.

Rarely an emotional person, his eyes were glossy.

'You should not speak to her again,' he said, standing over me, shaking his finger in my face like I was a high-school girl in trouble. 'Look at you!'

He was right. After what I'd just experienced, I realised, I was done. I knew in that moment it was time to let go. I wasn't letting go because I didn't love her. It was because I did, so much.

Without saying a word, I went over to where I'd put the record player proudly on display, the dead, droopy flowers – symbolic of my soul – on a nearby table. I picked them both up, and the Lewis Capaldi record. I took them outside and threw them on the patio while I grabbed a hammer from the shelves near the barbecue.

I swung the hammer over my head and brought it down with a ferocity I didn't know existed in me, meeting the pile of presents that lay haphazardly on the tiles with a huge C-R-A-C-K.

I smashed it all.

Then I went around the house, gathering up every piece of her that remained in my space, every little thing she'd ever left behind. Undies, socks, a phone charger, T-shirts . . . every photo, every handwritten note she'd ever left me – she used to like leaving them behind in secret places for me to find when she'd return home . . .

'I love you so much.'

'You're the most beautiful girl in the world.'

'Sophie Cachia, I really, really rate ya.'

'I promise I'll never stop loving you.'

These were things I never thought I'd throw away. But never underestimate the power of a backyard bonfire in a time of need. Saying a silent farewell as I lit a match, I watched as the flames burnt away the last pieces of our connection that I'd clung to so tightly. From that moment I knew, this was it. I needed to work on healing, not just for myself, but for my children.

I booked an appointment to see my GP at eight o'clock the next morning, and when I walked in, I simply said, 'I need help.' I told him what I had nearly done the night before and he put me straight onto a very strong antidepressant, referring me to a psychiatrist for the next steps of my healing journey. I made a pact with myself to get myself better. I'd allowed myself to endure too much hurt for too long, and I was done. I couldn't let it go on any longer.

~

Smashing and burning everything was incredibly cathartic, but I obviously wasn't healed after that. Far from it. But it was a moment of acceptance, at last, and a realisation of just how important it was for my health that I let her go. It didn't matter if I still loved her – this wasn't healthy for me. I deserved to be happy. I had to learn to allow simplicity to replace complexity.

I've spent a lot of time since then reflecting on myself and my behaviours, my part in the whole ordeal, and have realised just how different we are as people. I'm someone who needs to deal with things in order to process them. I need to speak about things, to cry, to put everything on the table, whereas it seems to me that she disconnects. It's part of what makes her such a successful athlete – her ability to focus on one thing and shut out the rest. It is the most incredible trait for a sportsperson. She was able to move across the world, away from her family, away from her girlfriend and shift focus to the job at hand. She wouldn't let anything distract her from her career, and good on her, I hope it brings longevity in her profession.

But that way of being in the world was so foreign to me – it's just not how I work, especially when I'd gone from being with Jaryd, who worked so well with me and alongside me, even in difficult times. We could always come together to figure out a solution and to work out how we were going to go about things, how we would move forward. We're still like that today; we're on the same team. We help each other and we work through things together, just as a strong, united team should.

With her departure, I felt like I had no control over my own life. I felt I had no say in how my time panned out; no say in how any of it was handled. I didn't get to make this decision that so deeply affected my life – it was a choice that was made for me. But like I said, we are just different people. While I want to talk things through, want to cry, want to take action, it seems that her way of coping was to disengage.

I don't know whether that is actually true or just my perception, but the only thing that gives me some kind of peace is telling myself that she must have been struggling, she must've been hurting too, and simply did what she had to do to get through. That thought process allowed me to get some sleep at night in those early days and weeks after the big blow-up.

My psychologist gave me an analogy that really reso-nated with me. She told me that some people, like myself, like to treat exes like a coffee table book. We leave them in the middle of our loungeroom where we can always appreciate their beauty, a memory we can pick up and flick through whenever we feel like a browse. Other people need to take that book and lock it away in the filing cabinet as a way of processing. An 'out of sight, out of mind' approach, unable to have it in front of their faces every day.

Maybe she'll read this and do her classic eye roll, say that it's not the case at all, that I was way off the mark; that she just didn't love me anymore. That happens in life; it's just the way things are sometimes. But I need to hold onto the belief that it was her coping mechanism because it's the only way I can give myself peace and clarity around the situation. Otherwise, my nightmare becomes a hurtful reality.

Moving on from her family was equally as heartbreaking for me. I felt like they, too, had become my family, like I'd known them forever, and I could see vividly how my life would've played out as a part of their united tribe. They had always been so welcoming, so accepting, and I felt a sense of belonging with them I'd never known before. I was mourning the loss of that future I had built in my mind; a future I would never have.

It's probably not spoken about enough that when you breakup with someone, you breakup with their entire life as well. It's not uncommon for your lover's friends and family members to become as important to you as the partner themselves. Countless happy memories together, a shared pride in the person you share, connections on all sorts of meaningful levels. Sometimes saying goodbye to them is just as difficult as saying goodbye to your partner in the wake of a devastating relationship breakup, but holding on is also self-defeating and only serves as a painful reminder of what will never be.

My focus had shifted to trying to stay afloat during Melbourne's longest stage-four lockdown. Family were unable to visit, nothing was open, I was home-schooling my two children every day (as well as managing their sense of loss for this person as best I could, too), and I could only leave my house for one hour a day to go for a walk or to the super-market. I had no escape from myself – I couldn't go out with my friends, I couldn't start a new hobby, I couldn't go to work . . . Every day was a painful soundtrack on repeat, while I was acutely aware that she seemed to be flourish-ing in a whole new environment. Exploring life in a new country with new teammates, going to training . . . she'd been thrown into an environment that allowed her to be distracted, worlds away from the stale grey existence I was trapped in.

Every day I had to sit there, alone with my thoughts, desperate to get away from them, to get out of my head.

'You need to learn to sit with your shit and stop running away from it.'

Blondie With The Bun had said that to me once, after I'd brushed her aside yet again to return to my turbulent love.

'You *never* just sit with your shit, Soph. You keep escaping it.'

She'd been so right from the beginning, and I hadn't been able to see it this whole time. For someone who thought she was so self-aware, I'd been pretty damn great at pushing away feelings of discomfort and ignoring negative feelings that came up. It'd been six months since Blondie and I had even spoken, yet she'd seen something in me back then that it took me being dragged through utter emotional hell to realise for myself.

Looking back, I believe it was all supposed to happen. Did it hurt like hell? Yes, it absolutely fucking did. But I believe the universe made me sit with my shit and confront a lot of stuff that I never had before. I was forced to learn to be on my own; to be okay with not speaking to anybody; to be fine not having sex, not having company . . . I used to always distract myself with things like that but in stage-four lockdown, when karma bit me in the ass, I had no choice but to learn that life lesson.

I was forced to sit with my shit, just like Blondie had said – and in doing so, I came to a place of enjoying my own company. I was okay on my own. In fact, I *liked* living by myself, just me and the kids. It had been a fucking brutal process, going to therapy and revisiting all of those suppressed moments – but I was so determined to get to a better headspace, and I did it.

Something had truly flipped in me. I didn't feel that sadness anymore and, for the first time *ever*, I didn't want her back. I obviously still loved her and I know a part of her will always be with me through life, but that intense yearning and desperation had moved on. I no longer felt like I needed her to make me feel something.

I will never apologise for loving her too hard. For continually fighting for what I wanted, for fighting for the love I knew existed and that connection I yearned for so deeply. Who I will apologise to, though, is myself – for staying too long somewhere I knew I shouldn't be. Countless times in life we are told to 'follow our heart' in the merciless battle of head versus heart. 'Your heart will always know the way,' we are told, 'and will take you to where you are supposed to end up.' But what if that heart is shattered into a thousand pieces? Then what? Which piece do we follow? What if, by following that heart, we destroy our brain – leaving no capacity for logical thinking when we need it the most?

All you can do is forgive yourself for loving so freely and set yourself free from all the reasons it didn't work out the way you hoped.

Chapter 22

There was one woman who had always been there for me when I needed her during my mental health struggles, who had always given me the time of day – although, like a coward, I had left her behind so thoughtlessly over and over again over the course of a year. For a long time, Blondie With The Bun had been telling me she thought I needed to be on some form of medication, that she thought I would benefit from regularly seeing a psychologist. So, when I was finally brave enough to start taking prescription medication, I wanted to let her know. Even though we hadn't seen each other or been in contact (aside from a beautiful bunch of flowers she'd sent me for my 30th the month before) I felt she was someone who would support me and appreciate this huge step I'd taken. Somewhere inside, I also knew I owed it to her as part of me taking ownership for my past actions.

I sent her a text. I told her about the blow-up, about the birthday present; I told her about the tree incident, how badly I'd wanted to hurt myself, about the other random gift of a Louis Vuitton wallet that showed up at my door the month after my ex told me to never contact her again. I told her that I had now made the conscious choice to move on from this, that I couldn't allow myself to live like that anymore, and that I was getting help.

'I just wanted to let you know that I finally bit the bullet. I'm seeing a psychologist,' I wrote, amongst other things – not expecting a reply, but wanting to finally confess that she had been right all along, and that I did need help.

She replied.

'At the end of the day, I want you healthy, I want you happy,' she wrote back, no anger or resentment evident for what I'd put her through. 'I'm so happy for you. But I also can't be a support person for you right now. I'm sorry.'

I completely understood. In fact, I was proud of her for putting that boundary in place, and maybe even a little relieved. In the past, we would have ended up falling back together so quickly, so naturally, which I know wouldn't have been good (or fair) for either of us at the time.

Another month or two went by and I slowly picked myself up and got my head back together. It wasn't fast or easy, but that healing was necessary. Going through treatment helped me look back on a lot of my actions and decipher what they meant and why I had acted in certain ways. I began to truly realise how badly I'd treated this amazing, kind woman and that, in so many ways, I had been doing to someone else what I felt was being done to me. I had been so okay to just call it off when it suited me and then go back to her when I wanted validation. I was so critical of the pain I was in, yet thought nothing of disregarding this woman who had treated me with so much love and kindness.

As I sat in the courtyard one day, sobbing with my head in my hands, I had an epiphany.

Oh my God . . . I get it now.

I now knew everything she went through, all because of me.

I grabbed my phone, tears still running down my cheeks, and typed out a message.

'I'm sorry for making you feel abandoned. I'm sorry I made you feel unimportant. I'm sorry if it looked like it was so easy for me to let go. I have felt that too and I get it now. I know exactly what it feels like, and I wouldn't wish that sense of abandonment upon anybody.'

Because it was, to date, the most difficult life experience I'd endured.

Now, I am a spiritual believer. I do believe in the power of fate and of the universe, and to this day I am certain that everything that had happened up until that point was divinely guided. Too many things that occurred simply could not be ignored. As shitty as it was, and though it was my toughest life experience, the reality is that I learnt a lot – and if I hadn't been through what I had, I would never have truly understood the sense of confusion and rejection that I put this poor girl through.

As someone who had loved ferociously and accepted someone back into my life countless times, it was *her* that had always done the same thing for me.

I didn't expect *anything* from her. I didn't once try to pursue her or ask her to take me back. It wasn't what I wanted, and even if I did, I'd come too far in my emotional development to risk hurting either her or myself again. I just needed her to know that I explicitly understood now what I'd done, the consequences of my actions, and that even if I never received an apology and acknowledgement myself, this girl deserved all of that from me.

But fate wasn't through with us yet – the universe had much more in store.

~

During that stage of lockdown in Melbourne, we weren't allowed to travel further than five kilometres from our homes and with this girl living on the other side of town, nearly an hour away, there was no way we were going to see each other as long as this lockdown was in place. So, you can imagine my surprise when I heard through our mutual friends that she was moving just two suburbs away from where I was living, a ten-minute drive. She was living in a serviced unit in Brunswick with a couple of her teammates, they told me, in the same chain of apartments their team management always booked – and that now put her firmly inside my allowed radius.

Surely we won't run into each other.

I mean, five kilometres . . . it's close but it's not that close.

The universe then revealed the next part of its plan. I had been referred to a new psychologist . . . whose practice was in Brunswick. It was on Sydney Road, which is a very long street, packed with heaps of shops, cafes, restaurants, offices. Usually buzzing, it was quieter than usual with lockdown going on. I was driving along, looking for the right number – late again and frazzled. Some things never change.

I found a park, fumbling with my keys, ready to jump out of the car when I glanced up.

Oh my God.

This was the apartment building she had just moved to. I couldn't fucking believe it. Out of the whole suburb, on this 24km-long road, she was living right next door to the one psychologist's office I would be attending weekly. I couldn't believe it.

You're really gonna do this to me, Universe?

After my appointment, I popped into the Woolworths behind the practice to grab a couple of groceries and the entire time I was inside, I couldn't stop thinking that this would be *her* supermarket. I had this overwhelming feeling that I would bump into her, reuniting in the bloody vegetable aisle or something! I was relieved when we didn't, but every week as I would head off to see my psychologist, the thought of her was again thrown in my face, and I couldn't help but feel the universe was trying to make us run into each other. We had *always* lived on complete opposite sides of the city and then, straight after the government brought in a five-kilometre radius, she was suddenly moved inside that bubble? Not just in the bubble, but right next door to my psychologist's office?! What were the odds? There was no way that was a coincidence.

We did get back in touch with each other soon after that (though via text message, not some random meeting in Woolies). We hadn't seen each other in months and while neither of us was itching to dive into a relationship, it was really nice to reconnect when we did. I instantly remembered how warm she was, how kind and sweet and funny, and it was so beautiful to have her back in my life, even if just as a friend.

One night while we were texting, I joked, 'So when are you going to invite me over to see the new apartment?' Mind you, I was in bed, in my pyjamas, nestled under the covers with Maccas – in no way angling for an invite.

'Haha never,' she replied.

We kept chatting, and as we were winding things down, I got a message that said, 'Apartment 503.'

Wait, is she for real?

'Are you serious?' I shot back.

. . .

'If you don't come now, I'll change my mind.'

I was shocked. It was honestly the last thing I'd expected. I'd just been joking around. I sat there, starting at my phone.

Wait, is this a good idea?

Is this the worst idea in the world?

Do I even want to go?

Yes. Yes, I did want to go, even though I didn't know why. I'd just had the shittest few months – maybe it would be good to just hang out with her and her housemate, who was there too; just to have the company. I leaped out of bed, scattering Maccas fries all over the doona, threw on my trackies and raced over.

We talked and talked until 4am. We spoke about how hurt she'd been when I left her six months ago after weeks of back and forth with another woman.

'How could you do that to me?' she asked at one point. 'I just don't understand how you could bounce between us like that . . .'

I told her how sorry I was for the pain I'd caused her, but I also backed myself, reminding her that I'd maintained complete transparency with her during that time.

'You have every right to be upset by what I did, I take ownership of that and am remorseful for the pain I caused. But I won't let you criticise the way my brain works,' I explained gently. 'We view situations differently. That's something I've really learnt about relationships – that while you might view certain behaviour as morally wrong, another person sees it in another light. So while those actions may have hurt you, and I apologise profusely for that, I've now learnt that you can't be judgemental of a person for their brain working differently. We are humans; we just aren't all wired the same.

'At the time, that's what I needed to do,' I shrugged. 'You don't know what it's like to have been locked down in a ten-year relationship, to be a mum at 22, to be married and raising kids while other 20-somethings are out on adventures, dating, living their lives. So I am not apologising for that, for needing a little bit of time to explore and experiment. I hurt other people along the way – I even hurt myself with some of my actions. But I am so sorry that you were hurt in that process.'

The fact was, I'd fallen in love with someone, she'd abruptly left me, and then I met someone else . . . and then the first person came back. Finding myself in such an indecisive position wasn't intentional on my part. We'd met at a time in my life that was riddled with confusion.

'I just couldn't do that to someone,' she had said, anguish and accusation in her eyes over me having sexual relations with two people around the same time.

'I understand that' I said. 'But I am *not you.*'

They were tough conversations – the type of conversations I probably owed to her a lot earlier, if I'd had an adequate explanation to provide to her at the time. But these conversations were necessary so she could see the inner struggle I'd never really opened to her about. I think she finally saw the woman in me who had felt caged, tied down, and who had felt like she wasn't living an authentic life. She finally understood the stress and the anxiety I'd been grappling with, from the moment those first feelings of wanting to leave my marriage ever came into my head. How many people I felt like I was going to let down by leaving my husband – my family, my friends, above all my children . . . I discussed with her the excruciating guilt that I still live with every day for separating from their dad, for 'breaking up my family', and I think she was able to see a completely different, more vulnerable side to me; it perhaps helped her to understand *why* I had to do some of the things I did.

In my work with my psychologist and through the self-reflection I'd done over several months, I had also realised that a lot of the appeal with the other woman had been the sense of escape I found when I was with her. I did genuinely love her, but being able to jump on a plane and leave my life here for five days and go to a game or out for cocktails freely and spontaneously, go out for fancy dinners, go on real dates in a city where I didn't know anybody . . . that was so enticing and it was fulfilling a need that hadn't been met in a very long time – if ever. I'd felt so smothered in my life, for years and thanks to a multitude of factors, and what she seemed to offer was a chance to break free. It's not that I didn't love my children – of course I did, more than anything – but I was a woman who needed time on her own. She provided me with that time. I'd been totally respons-ible from a very young age, been a bloody good wife, with dinner on the table, looking after my man, his world, and everything to do with the kids, and the free spirit in me just needed to break away. Some people might go partying and take drugs in search of a thrill, some might travel, but for me, it was dating someone who gave me the opportunity to unpin my 'mum' badge and leave it behind for a little while. Someone who let me just be Sophie. It was exciting. For the first time in over six years – since having my son – I could just feel like . . . me.

Hindsight has taught me that it wasn't ever going to be sustainable. I could only run away for so long.

And then – while I was busy working to put myself back together again, not even looking for love – there was *her*.

The one who had initially scared me because of how perfect she was for my future. The one I ran from because she offered everything I'd convinced myself that I *didn't* want. The one who always welcomed me with open arms, with warmth and love. The one with the beautiful soul who would always listen, who held space for my fears and faults, the one who would *never* hurt me.

When we were first dating – in those very early days while I was still trading back and forth between the two women – I could so easily see our future together. I saw certainty and I saw commitment with her; I saw a comfortable, reassuring life together and it scared the shit out of me. I was terrified that we would settle down quickly – too quickly – and that I would run again, like I did from my marriage. In a way, I feel like everything had to play out exactly the way it did so that we could end up where we did; so I could learn to truly appreciate the value in that beautiful, calm existence.

~

I'm sure there are people who think we only got back together because my ex left, but that simply wasn't the case. We didn't get back together instantly – there were a good six months there where I was single and doing my own healing, and even when we did reconnect, there was a lot of back and forth, a lot of time spent together debating if this was the right thing, if it's what we wanted. She actually had to go away for a couple of months pretty much straight after we'd started speaking again – we probably only spent a week together before she had to go up to Queensland and when she left, we had absolutely no idea what was going to happen. We barely even talked about it, allowing the universe to let things play out naturally. We were both really aware that we'd only been back in touch for a week or so, it was a long time that she'd be gone, and we'd just touch base again when she got back. But neither of us could ignore the magnetism between us, the kind that had always been evident. After those excruciating few months following my breakup, it was her that reminded me all over again what happiness felt like.

When the borders opened up around mid-December, 2020, I took a flight to Queensland the next day. We weren't even officially back together, but Melbourne had been in lockdown for nearly six months at that stage, and now that I could finally jump on a plane and go to Queensland to watch her play, I was absolutely going to be there. I couldn't wait to see her again. I'd had time on my own, and whilst we were still in conversation, I just felt so at peace with the situation. I'd handed over the reins to her completely, allowing her to choose the next move as she was the one whose feelings had been always impacted.

Fear showed up before I could fully commit to being there – was travelling to visit her whilst still unsure of my feelings the smartest of moves to make? – so I talked to Jaryd about it and, as always, he knew what to say.

'I don't know if I should go because I don't know how I feel about her yet and I don't want to give her the wrong impression,' I told him – and I'd been very honest with her about that, too. She felt the same way; she didn't want to dive straight in as she was still dealing with a lot from our past, too.

'Soph, are you happy right now?' Jaryd asked me outright.

'Does she make you smile?

'Do you feel good?'

Yes, yes and yes.

'If she does, then go. You have been through so much in the past twelve months. I've seen you at rock bottom, so if you have a chance now to go and smile and laugh and have a good time, to go out for dinner, go watch some basketball and have fun, just fucking go.'

He was right. I did deserve to be happy, and I deserved to hang out with people that made me feel that way.

Too long, the Sophie in my previous life had ignored the signs when hanging around the wrong type of people and I'd made a promise to myself to pay attention to those who simply made me feel *good*. Who made life fun, who I enjoyed myself around, who made me laugh, and who added positive value to my life.

So I went.

I visited her a few times in December, and she even invited me to bring the kids along once, a contrast to what I'd previously known – something always so important to me, having my children so warmly accepted with open arms. When she came back to Melbourne just before Christmas, we naturally and so easily fell into this beautiful rhythm of life together.

I found myself at my kitchen bench one morning, washing the brekkie dishes and thinking about how we hadn't argued for a few weeks. Why did it feel strange?

Oh my God. This is . . . normal.

I was so surprised by the feeling of peace and calm, and I realised I'd become so used to the tension, angst and fighting in relationships that I thought it was the norm.

But this was good.

Like . . . *really* good.

I'd been running from this idea of 'normal' for so long, but after the ups and downs I had been through over the past year, I realised that 'normal' was exactly what I needed. 'Normal' had scared me for so long – I feared that if I found 'normal' again, I'd run like I had so many times in the past. But 'normal' no longer needed to be frightening. Coming home on a weeknight to sit on the couch and watch TV with a cup of tea next to someone I loved . . . That's all I wanted to do. I'd come full circle in the realisation that I was ready for that peace, that calm and that stability in my life.

Everything I truly wanted was in *her.*

Chapter 23

My girlfriend and I are living the most beautiful life together – actually, she's not my girlfriend anymore, she's my fiancée – but we've certainly both had to make some adjustments along the way. For one thing, apart from those five or so weeks with my ex, I've never lived with anyone except Jaryd. And for her, living with and essentially parenting children was a big step. She's obviously amazing with the kids, but there's a big difference between being good with them and living with them . . . whilst also trying to get what we both want out of a relationship.

I remember her telling me early into living together, in the middle of the day one time that she was tired, so she was going to go have a nap.

'What do you mean?!' I asked, shocked and, to be honest, a little bit horrified. 'You don't nap in the middle of the day when you've got kids at home. I haven't napped in seven years!'

She'd lived on her own, on and off, for seven years, so of course it seemed perfectly reasonable to go and have a little sleep in the middle of the day if she felt like it. But for me, as a mum of two young kids, I laughed at the idea. Who was she kidding?

Things like that are funny to look back on, because we certainly had to adjust to each other and I had to remind myself that, even though she was incredible with Bobby and Floss, it was *very* new to her. Often, I had to just breathe and remind myself that this was just as much an adjustment for her as it was for me – someone who'd spent a long time on her own running her household as she wished. Not that I needed her to 'mother' my children, but my boundaries were now set very firmly: that if she was to come into their home, she would come into their lives, and every aspect that that encompassed – and that responsibility was something that she needed to be aware that she was signing up for as she signed up to me, again.

When my ex had left, my children were devastated, especially Bobby. My son was asking where she was, why she didn't FaceTime them before bed anymore . . . How does a parent answer questions like that? I was destroyed at being left by someone I loved so dearly, but as a mother, I had my children's sadness and confusion to face up to as my first priority. And to be fair, it was probably my mistake in allowing her to become so deeply enmeshed in their lives – I can't put that blame on her – but regardless, I *couldn't* let it happen again. So, when Blondie and I were in talks of getting back together, I made it very clear from the outset that this was a deal breaker and that I could no longer involve my children in another blurred boundary of commitment.

'If you are in, you're all in,' I told her. 'There's no half-in, half-out. If we're doing this, you're in, and we are a family. My children deserve stability.'

I knew that by committing to her, I was committing my kids to her as well. But I was also laying the law down for myself. There would be no coming in and out again; no questions around whether I was sure or not. I knew that if I was going to do this, I was doing it properly – for her sake, for my sake and for my children's sake.

So I made that commitment to her, as she did to me, and here we are – living a wonderful life as a big modern family. To be brutally honest, the idea of giving someone something like a ring to symbolise love or equate to a relationship status makes me feel a little uneasy. Another 'tradition' that for so long we have been told is 'what we have to do', and I didn't realise how I felt about it until after my separation with Jaryd. I did face a moral dilemma, however, upon many discussions with Maddie. It wasn't fair for me to take that moment away from her, something that was important to her and that she wanted out of life – just because I had 'done it before' and my feelings surrounding it had changed. That's part of growing together as a couple and compromising in a relationship. Just because it didn't matter to me, it was significant for my partner – and therefore that now meant it was important to me, too.

Proposing to her – just us two – in the bedroom of our new home, renovation still in the process, and telling her how much I couldn't wait to grow our own family memories here one day, was such a beautiful moment. She had taken on so much coming into a relationship with my children, a life in which it's difficult to have your own time. She deserved her moment, her big moment in life she'd always dreamed of, and in that point in time, I knew I was making the exact right decision.

Our relationship has the usual ebbs and flows of life, many things we are still working on daily. A focus of mine now when approaching relationships is to look at the bigger picture and to not be so focused on the 'bad', but instead the many 'good' parts of life together. My approach to perspective and how it's you that chooses how you're going to view a situation has honestly changed my life. Your perspective is your version of reality, so by continually and consciously choosing to focus on 'what's bad' or 'what doesn't work' within your own dynamic – you're creating a very dark, dim reality for yourself to live out. Like any relationship, I could quickly list you five things she does that shits me to tears. But I also don't have to look far to know all the things she gives me. With her, it's never been about anything but her.

I live a pretty cool life. I have impressive work and career experiences, I can travel when and where I like, I earn a lucrative income and have many assets to my name. I don't need material things from her, nor do I want them from her. Her greatest gift to me is when she is simply herself. The easy-going, nurturing country girl that everyone loves. I call her 'my calm' because she has absolutely taught me what it is like to be calm and centred in my life. When everything else is go-go-go, she makes chilling on the couch in PJs my most favourite experience. She allowed my life to become soothing and assured, and never once have I questioned where I stood with her. While we 'ummed' and 'aaahed' over whether we should get back together or not, when we did, I was so peaceful, in a blissful bubble of appreciation and acceptance.

But it wasn't just her that made me happy again.

I'd finally come to a place where I was at peace with myself as well. If we'd gotten back together in August, as soon as my ex had left the country, it would have been for all the wrong reasons. It would have been because I just needed that validation, a top-up for my ego, but I had to learn to be alone and to be okay with it, and I had to go through those really intense emotions alone.

I was scared of hurting her again, though, and in all transparency – part of me still is. I think I will live with the fear of hurting people forever. Where I am currently at, I believe I will live with that fear of commitment forever – a sign at how tough the 'amicable separation' with Jaryd was on me. When I married that man, I promised forever because I *believed* forever. And the speed with which that unravelled around me has left a piece of my heart locked away that I'm not sure I'll ever be able to give to anyone ever again. I acted in ways to protect myself, but I refuse to live in fear, which would ultimately mean denying myself a life of fulfilment and experience. No relationship is ever guaranteed but accepting that we cannot control the uncontrollable allowed me to move towards her again.

I approach life now with an empowering sense of realism – flexible to the ups and downs, fluid in the face of disappointments that may come along, accepting that they are all part of life and further shaping who we are. Welcoming relationships when they come and allowing them to go when they've run their course – never taking away from the role and importance that a person has played in your story. Accepting that we're happy now, we're enjoying life together, and whatever happens in the future, we will face it. Life is good.

The baby question comes up a lot for me, too, and to be honest, it fucking scares me – for many of the same reasons that having a baby should have probably scared me at 22, had I not been naive, madly in love and desperate to become a mother.

At the time of writing this book, I'm suffering yet another internal battle; an intense, paralysing fear and the fact that I am actually *desperate* to have another baby. But what if we were to break up again one day, and then I've got kids with two broken families? That thought frightens me to my core. I want another baby, so, so much. But this crippling fear is standing in the way. It's not that I don't want a baby with my partner because she would be the most incredible mum and the most *stunning* pregnant woman – I tell her this all the time. I would love for her to see *me* with babies because I feel like being a mum is what I was put on earth to do, and I would *love* to do it with her. But I can't hide the worries that I have around it due to my life experience. I love my partner, but whilst sounding like I am completely contra-dicting myself, I do live now with knowledge that life can change abruptly and that children will feel any of your pain through life.

If I could have been pregnant six months ago, I would have. The only reason I'm not? I live with a lot of anxiety around the fact that I'm just not quite sure if my environ-ment is right for that just now, because my fear of 'what if it doesn't work out?' is creating an immense amount of pressure for me.

It's ironic, isn't it? That these fears contradict my message for this entire book? But when there are children involved, I now know you have to be so, so careful. It's not just my life that would be affected by the introduction of a new baby or a possible relationship breakdown. I live knowing that I'll be fine no matter what. If my partner and I did decide to have a baby one day and we were to part later down the track, I know I'll be fine . . . but what about this child? How do you make that decision for someone's future? Is it fair to bring a child in when there's uncertainty? And is this uncertainty something I'm going to feel forever due to my past? Is it natural for me to feel like that having separated once before?

If I was on my own right now, I would comfortably have a baby by myself. If I could do it on my own, I'd be pregnant right now – raising my family in my own little bubble. I'd be sitting here with my baby, and it's *my* baby. Sounding selfish and incredibly unfair to my partner? No. It's me pushing people away to protect those I love. A baby on my own makes the most sense currently. That way, no one else gets hurt in the process. The baby's not living between two homes; there's no risk of my partner getting hurt. I'm not able to let anyone down again.

But I am with a woman and I love a woman, and we talk about children and I want to give her that life. My uncertainty truly has nothing to do with her or us, it's all about my own insecurities around letting people down again. I love my relationship and I love my partner, but I have a fear of committing to someone long-term with children because of the separation I went through with Jaryd. Whilst things with us are amazing now, and what we have is great, I know how much I struggled internally when I did begin to start having doubts about my marriage. When those thoughts came in, they were totally out of my control. I knew I was falling out of love – that I was having a change of mind, a change of heart – yet I was helpless to stop it happening, regardless of how much I knew my decisions were going to impact my children's lives.

Life has shown me that you can love someone more than you've ever loved anyone else and you can have a blissful life with them, but that can change at any time. My uncertainty isn't about her or us – it's about whether or not I want to take that risk when I don't know what's coming next. So many things in life are completely out of our control and it is terrifying to think about other people – children – being affected by my choices. But I also can't be a slave to that mindset my whole life, because I know I would be limiting myself. I could be missing out on so much happiness.

Chapter 24

It does take a very special person to come into a dynamic like Jaryd and I have these days – and my partner is 100 per cent that very special person.

She sees beauty in the family connection Jaryd and I have created and the way we parent together as a united team now. Whenever he comes to get the kids, he knows everyone's coffee orders and he always brings us one, stays for a chat. We are all family – and he and I will *always* be family. And the gorgeous partner Jaryd has now brought into our circle – one who is not threatened by the strength of our connection; one who sees it simply for what it is – has only made our family unit stronger.

Very early on, when we were first discussing separating, Jaryd and I made a pinky promise that we would have a 'no dickheads' policy when it came to dating. If either of us was seeing someone who had any issue with how we run things, they didn't get to come into our lives. It just wouldn't work because we wouldn't allow this dynamic to change, for the sake of our kids and for the sake of our whole family unit. People tried to warn me that things might change if and when Jaryd got a girlfriend, but I wanted nothing more than for Jaryd to be happy and for there to be another extended member of our family – and I couldn't be happier for him to now have that, to have found the same love that I have. For my kids to have another incredible woman in their life, another role model to lean on and be guided by; another person to love them. How could that possibly be seen as a negative?

My good friend's mum who's gay has really inspired and driven the way Jaryd and I have decided to shape our lives, because I grew up in my twenties watching the way this incredible woman and her ex-partner navigate their own family dynamic. They split up when my friend was around ten or eleven, and coming from a big Lebanese family, it wouldn't have been a surprise if the mum had been ostracised for leaving her husband to chase love with a woman. But it didn't go that way – it was the total opposite and my friend's mum and dad are best friends still to this day. She's never once had to doubt her place within that loving family. They always said it didn't matter that they weren't married anymore; it didn't matter that they didn't have those rings on their fingers. They were family.

Jaryd and I, aware of life's unpredictability and the roller-coaster ride it can take you on, always said if we ever broke up, that's how we wanted to be – Mum, Dad and our partners all sitting around having a laugh, with nothing but love and respect for everyone around. It's quite ironic that our life did, in fact, follow the same path, mimicking these people whose devotion to love and family, however it looks, inspired us for so many years.

I'm not naive to the fact that this isn't possible in every situation. When there's cheating, abuse, betrayal, people end up hating each other – that does happen, and I am very aware that Jaryd and I are so incredibly blessed that we actually still really like each other as people. We're still so in tune with each other on an emotional level, but it's not a romantic love anymore. Some people have even joked, 'Oh you two are still together, you just don't have sex with each other,' but what we have has developed well beyond romance. In fact, I probably see him as more like my brother – someone I want to support in every life endeavour, where nothing he could tell me would ever make me turn against him. I am as close to him as I am to my mum, my dad, my sisters. Likewise, our families will always be family, too – connected by two little angels going by the names of Bobby and Florence. I will forever call my father-in-law 'Dad', Jaryd's sister and his brother are forever my sister and brother as well, and he'll never lose my mum as his devoted mother-in-law. We are always supporting each other's happiness, no matter how that looks, from the day our lives started to head in different directions, until the day we die. That is nothing short of beautiful and I am forever grateful for my life.

I see some people dealing with absolute asshole partners and I am thankful every day that I met Jaryd. No, our marriage didn't work out, but our friendship did. Our lives did. Our children did. Our respect for each other will outlive any marriage certificate. I've got two beautiful children with the most incredible dad. Society wants to tell us that that's failure, but how have we failed? We have to start shifting that narrative and I am determined to do that for my children. We need to celebrate the intent behind marriage, because *intending* to spend your life with someone is itself a massive achievement – as is couples respectfully realising that they've come as far as they could as one. Both deserve praise.

Jaryd and I always agreed that we could have stayed together. It would not have been us though, because it goes against what we both believe in: living your true life and being your authentic self. Whilst our grandparents would've probably thought us staying together was the way to provide our kids with the best life, I completely disagree. We are giving the kids their best life by doing this. We are showing them what it looks like to live a happy, fulfilled life as individuals stepping away from each other in order to come together in different ways.

I want them to see their mama, the mama who took a chance, who was willing to take risks in life. A mama who was not afraid to make mistakes – one who shows them that growth can be painful and change can be scary, but not as scary and painful as staying somewhere you know you don't want to be.

'Do you want to risk holding on for too long?' Jaryd and I had asked each other. 'Do we risk ending up miserable and tense together? Or do we go our separate ways and see what happens?'

When we did initially break up, we honestly didn't go into it thinking we were done for good, that we'd never get back together. We were genuinely taking some time to explore and live apart, to see how it played out. We would have loved it if, a few years down the track, we reunited, but we were also very aware that that may not happen.

As it turned out, the freedom we allowed each other to have ended up coming at exactly the right time.

I'm also so proud that we're raising our kids to be such open-minded, accepting and loving people. The environment I grew up in was not one I would call homophobic, but I can see now that I did lead a very sheltered existence for most of my life, so it's extremely important to me – and to Jaryd – that our kids are raised exposed to every type of unique human to walk this earth. I want them to see that nothing is off limits in life, that the choices and possibilities are there to create, and they are endless. And I certainly don't want to rob them of their queerness; something that I feel society did to me.

To that end, we've been very open with all types of humans since my kids were born. Bobby and Florence have been surrounded by wonderful gay friends of ours since they were born, so they know no different in their upbringing, and it's not as if I have to introduce them some mysterious LGBTQIA+ world because it's happening all around them – it's just a normal part of life as they know it. We've always been very open about the fact that girls can kiss girls, boys can kiss boys; men can marry each other; boys can wear dresses and can want to live life as a female . . . and that all of that is not only okay, it's great. It's normal.

It's incredible to see how accepting Bobby is. When all the kids at school were saying they had girlfriends, one day, he said he had a boyfriend instead. Whether or not he did, I don't know, but his home environment has let him understand how okay that was and gave him the confidence to say it to his peers. My son is just incredible at being so open-minded. I honestly think he was born that way, which is beautiful, but I also believe that we, as parents, have instilled in him this absolute inherent acceptance of everyone. I am also proud of the acceptance I am now seeing from my daughter – day by day, she is understanding that one can choose to live life however they please, and not just what she sees on TV.

Obviously, seeing me with female partners goes a long way to normalising every kind of relationship, too, and it has always been so important to me to be honest from the start. I've had three actual girlfriends and whenever they were first introduced to the kids, I didn't try to hide what those relationships were or twist the truth in any way. I would tell the kids, 'This is Mummy's girlfriend and Mummy loves her.' The first relationship I had with a woman – who is now one of my good friends – was very open and fluid, and while we didn't use labels, I didn't want to confuse the kids, so they knew she was someone very important in our house and that she was very special and, again, that Mummy loved her. I don't believe children need a lot of labels to understand what's going on. They just need to know they are safe and that the people around them love them and love each other.

I've also been very honest with the kids when relationships have ended, because they have seen when I am hurt, watched as I've cried, and they deserve to know what is causing Mummy pain – and why these people that they have come to love, too, are suddenly never there. So I'd tell them, 'I know we really loved spending time with this person, but they won't be coming over anymore because our relationship ended.'

I remember Bobby saying to me once, 'Did you broked up?'

'Yes, baby, we broked up,' I told him.

'You crying 'cause you broked up? Did she dump you?'

Ouch, babe.

'Yes, she did.'

The impact that this has had on my kids is something I was so fearful about when Jaryd and I were deciding to separate and I was about to explore my sexuality. I remember crying to him in the car and I wasn't crying for me, I was crying for my children; for the fact that decisions I was making would affect them. Were my children going to get bullied at school because of a choice I made? It was really difficult because I wanted to explore this part of myself I'd never known existed, and I wanted to be that example for my children, to encourage them to live life and own who they are . . . But at the same time, I didn't want Bobby and Florence getting picked on because, 'Your mum's a lesbian, your mum's a lesbian.'

But with the direction we've chosen to raise our children, I am confident that they will simply say 'Yeah? So what?', shrug their shoulders and run off to play.

Bobby had a few of his little friends sleep over for his birthday last year and I popped them into my and my partner's bed to watch a movie. While I was turning on the TV, one of them asked me, 'Who sleeps in here?'

'Maddie and I sleep in here,' I replied.

'Oh! Why do you and Maddie sleep here?'

''Cause they're gay,' said Bobby very casually.

'Yeah, they're girlfriends,' said another friend with a shrug. (This was before we got engaged, obviously!)

'Oh, okay cool.'

And that was it. No giggling or whispering, no cries of, 'Eww, yuck!' They just turned on *The Addams Family* and as they were watching it, I realised, we are doing something so good here. I'm so excited for the next generation after hearing that conversation and so proud of Bobby and his little group of seven-year-old mates.

Yep. We're doing something right.

Chapter 25

Going on a reality TV show isn't something I ever planned for myself, but on the back of everything I'd been through over the past few years, it's what life threw my way at the end of 2021. Around September, I was preparing to head into one of the most highly applied-for reality game shows in the world: *Survivor*. It's one of my all-time favourite shows, I've loved it ever since I was a little girl. I remember being around nine years old and when my mum thought I was in bed, I'd sneak out to the back lounge room and watch those early American seasons. I've literally watched every season – not one I've ever missed – and I know all the cast members, I know the game back to front.

I'd never even considered actually going on the show, though, as being a self-proclaimed princess when it comes to the outdoors is in my blood. I've never been one to go on rides (even now at 31, you won't get me on a Ferris wheel) and I'm quite content to never write 'adrenaline junkie' in my Tinder bio. I like my feet on the ground, I like comfort, and I own my sookiness when it comes to my fear of certain crawly creatures. So when I first got a call in late 2019 asking me to go on *Survivor*, it started as a big joke between myself and my colleagues and friends.

Before I got that phone call, though, I'd recently gone through another life-changing event that had shifted my entire outlook on my world – and as a result, my thoughts around the opportunity began to shift the more I considered it.

I had never been able to travel without Jaryd since my diagnosis with post-natal depression in 2014. He was my security blanket. I developed an extreme fear of flying and even the thought of being in a hotel room up in Sydney on my own for a work trip was a petrifying thought. I would get anxiety if I was ever on my own; I couldn't sleep without my children next to me. I physically needed people around me – I didn't like being on my own because I would get so into my own dark thoughts that I'd create a panic within my own brain. It sounds crazy, and maybe I was for a while there, but when you're in it, suffocating, it is terrifying. So if

I ever had to go away, even just to Sydney for a day trip for work, most of the time Jaryd would come with me, and if he didn't, I'd have to be highly medicated because I just couldn't function existing on my own in those moments.

But at around the time all these huge changes started happening in my life, and Jaryd and I started to make some decisions about what we were doing and where our relationship was going, I decided to take Bobby for a holiday – just me and him having some mum-son time. It sounds random, but it wasn't completely. I'd been inspired after talking to one of Jaryd's aunties, who has a tradition of taking each of her teenage children on a solo bonding trip every year. She was happily married but very independent and she and her husband were really cool, fun, super-adventurous people – and these trips they took didn't necessarily have to be anything extravagant, but she shared with me that the bonding time she had with each child was really special. It was important for her to have those individual life experiences with each of her children.

I really loved the idea that they'd go and create these amazing memories together, and I wanted to have that for my children and my life, too.

It also stemmed from the fact that I'd never had the chance to really travel either. Whilst all my friends were doing Contikis and packing up and moving to London, I was at home changing nappies – and yes, the thought of doing it scared the shit out of me, but I lived with a lot of regret that I'd never solo-travelled at all. It was time.

'I think I want to go somewhere with Bobby when he's five,' I told Jaryd one night in early 2019, with Bobby's birthday fast approaching.

Jaryd, of course, supported the idea. So the next night at the dinner table, I said to Bobby, 'Mummy wants to take you on a holiday. Where is somewhere in the world you want to go? You can choose anywhere, just you and me.'

He paused to think for only a minute.

'Japan,' said my then-four-year-old.

'Why Japan?'

'I like eating sushi!'

So I looked into it the very next day, knowing I would develop an intense amount of anxiety around being a woman travelling on her own with a child. Yet, after a lot of research and feedback from others who'd done it, I discovered that Japan is a really safe place to travel. Within a few days, Bobby and I went to the travel agency where a friend of mine worked and we booked a trip, right there on the spot. Handing over my card and paying for it so quickly was a pretty big thing for me, because it was *real* after that; it was happening, whether I liked it or not. I was one step closer than I'd ever been to this kind of adventure. It was something I – the previous Sophie – had never been able to fathom possibly doing, but here I was doing it. We were doing it.

My mum really didn't get it when I told her.

'What do you mean?' she asked when I told her my exciting news. 'What about Florence? She's only a baby!'

'Well, Mum, she'll be at home with her dad so she'll be fine,' I replied.

'But why are you leaving her out?'

My mum struggled to understand that I would do the same thing for Floss when she turned five; that I would let her pick somewhere to go and we'd have a trip, just the two of us. She couldn't quite comprehend why we weren't all going as a family, why I'd want to do something for myself. It was just a generational thing, I know, but I wish she'd said something like, 'Oh that's amazing, Soph! Go for it!', rather than questioning my motives and reminding me of the responsibilities here, like I was doing something wrong.

In the days leading up to the trip, I had severe anxiety. I would cry hysterically, I kept wondering if I should just cancel the whole thing. Even the night before I was completely hysterical and riddled with fear of making such a huge move in my life.

'I can't do this,' I sobbed to Jaryd. 'I can't do it.'

He was my biggest supporter, as always.

'Go, Soph, it's going to be amazing.'

He was always so positive.

Saying goodbye to two-year-old Florence was difficult – my anxiety was choking me high in my throat, suffocating me until the moment I walked through the gate. We scanned our passports and then it was just me and Bobby. And in that instant, I went from anxious mess to survival mode. It was the challenge I knew I needed to grow.

Now you are in control. You are in charge. There is no one here to help you.

So get your shit together and let's go have this amazing trip.

The second the family was gone, and it was just Bobby and me walking through the international airport, I went into protection mode – powerful mum mode – and I thought, *We are going to do this, buddy.* There was no turning back.

~

Our flight was due to land at Tokyo really late at night so I'd spoken to my travel agent about how we would get from the airport to our accommodation.

'It'll be fine,' she assured me. 'When you walk out of the airport, there's a big bus and train station. You just jump on a train, and it'll take you straight to your hotel, it's so easy.'

After making our way through immigration, we walked out of the gates – me dragging two giant suitcases while Bobby carried his own little case, plus a backpack – and approached the busiest bus/train stop I've even seen in my life. Every sign was in Japanese. Not one word of English anywhere. Hundreds of people busily making their way to their transport.

Oh, fuck.

This is where Jaryd would usually step in and take control of the situation. Whenever we'd gone anywhere, he took care of us. He was 'the protector', and if anything went wrong, it was always going to turn out fine because Jaryd was there to sort it out. But this time, he wasn't there. This was all up to me. At this point I normally would have burst into tears, freaking out about what we were going to do. But again, I had no choice. And it's exactly why I had put myself in this position.

Right. You can do this, Soph. You're going to figure this out.

I was going from bus terminal to bus terminal, trying to read the maps and signs, showing my itinerary to every bus driver who pulled up (mind you, it was in English, so not at all helpful . . .). I knew the hotel was near Disneyland and found someone who knew enough English to tell me that trains and buses to the amusement park had stopped for the night . . .

Fuck! Bigger fuck!

Obviously I knew that I could get a taxi if I needed to, I knew that we would get there eventually. But reality hit very quickly that I had to figure this out on my own. And I did. I did work it out. We had to change buses halfway there, but we made it, and I rang Jaryd immediately, ecstatic that I'd done it on my own. That was only the first day and I knew it was going to be such a good trip because Sophie from two years earlier could never have done what I had just done.

What might appear to be a fairly standard travel experience was me putting my then-self in my worst real-life nightmare. When you've suffered with severe anxiety your whole life and you have constantly relied on others to be your security and your comfort, stepping out by yourself in an airport on the other side of the world, with no one who is able to help you, not able to speak the language – not to mention having an exhausted five-year-old in tow, who's just sat on a plane for eleven hours and needs food, toilet and bed – well, that's a huge accomplishment. It was an empowering moment and the beginning of me discovering the Sophie that was inside.

We spent twelve days traveling around Japan. We started in Tokyo and caught fast trains to Osaka and Kyoto. Kyoto was one of my favourite places to visit because we were staying in a very quiet area near these vibrant night markets, and it just had a really calm vibe – one I never thought I'd experience with the anxiety that I had suffered for so long. There was something so sweet about Kyoto as a city that Bobby and I would walk the streets till 11 o'clock at night, buying food from market stalls and really taking in the culture, and not once did I ever feel unsafe.

We did all the essential kid activities – Universal Studios and Disneyland. We went to these crazy cafes with cats and monsters . . . clearly a focus in my planning was to provide Bobby with some memorable experiences. But I did decide I wanted to take one day for me, to do some temple tours and see the bamboo forests, so I hired a tour guide to take us around. She met us in the lobby and the three of us had breakfast together before we headed out to see the sites. About halfway through the day, three or four hours into the one-on-two tour, Bobby tugged at my sleeve.

'Mum, why does this lady not stop talking? She's so annoying, why won't she stop speaking to us?'

It still makes me laugh out loud to this moment. He had no idea that she was a tour guide I'd hired and she was simply doing her job. He thought we'd just picked up a stranger at breakfast!

'That's her job darling,' I laughed. Poor thing!

Seeing and experiencing Japanese culture was pure magic, and I made sure that Bobby and I dived deep into it where we could. But none of that is what I really took away from the trip. It was the bonding opportunity with my son. The one-on-one chats on our train rides. Learning more about each other as every day passed. The pride I had seeing him walk so far in one day. It was the empowerment of seeing that, yes, I can do this on my own. It was the independence that began to grow within.

Watching my son adapt and gain his own independence let me know again that this trip was life changing. Bobby was a star the whole trip, carrying his own things and never once complaining. I have a photo of him at a very busy train station, his backpack full, his heavy suitcase in his hand, and he's carrying it up about a hundred steps. He did it because he had to; because I had a backpack of my own and two big suitcases. He had no choice but to step up, just like his mama did. Normally, if we're at home and I ask him to help with the shopping out of the car or something, he'll say, 'Nooo Mum, it's too heavy,' as most five-year-olds would. But in that moment, Bobby instinctively knew he had no choice but to carry his own suitcase, that he needed to play his part and help Mama with the load in order to get to where we needed to go, and it was a really moving thing to witness. He didn't complain once, not once, on the whole trip. And again, it's because neither of us had a choice. We knew we had to do it and we had to do it together. And I think that's a poignant theme both from the trip and in life – you're going to get through it. No matter how far it seems you have to climb, or how heavy the load may feel, you've just got to get on with it and you *will* make it through.

I came back from that trip a totally different person. I proved to myself that I *can* be alone. I *can* raise my children on my own. I can work. I can travel. I can be financially independent. I proved to myself that *I could do it all.*

I learnt so much about the significance of Buddhism and lotus flowers during my travels there, and returned to have a design of both tattooed on my arm, blending the powerful symbols of enlightenment. I took inspiration of rebirth and new existence from Buddhism and combined it with the lotus flower – revered for its ability to bloom into a pure, gorgeous flower, despite rising from dirty water.

That trip was in 2019, a year when there were obviously plenty of other life-altering things going on for me and my identity. But without that experience, I wouldn't be the woman I am today – and I certainly wouldn't have said 'yes' to going on *Survivor* two years later.

~

Soon after Bobby and I returned home, my management team came to me with an opportunity that I never could've imagined myself doing in the past. They knew people that worked with *Survivor* who wanted me to go on the show. My instant reaction was, 'Fuck no.' Like I said, I'm usually a sook in terms of things like cold weather, being tired, bugs and spiders (all jokes aside, I suffer from severe arachnophobia). In the past, I've simply avoided doing things that scared me. I've never liked going too far out in the ocean because I'm scared I'll either drown or get eaten by a shark, for instance, or I wouldn't go on a ride in case it breaks and I die and I end up on the front page of the papers because the carousel blew up . . . you know, ridiculous things like that. It's just how I've always been and I'm okay with it.

But it was the thought of being away from people with absolutely no contact that terrified me the most. I've always had my safety blankets around me. For such a long period of time, Jaryd was my safety blanket and after we separated, my children became my safety blanket, so *Survivor* is something I would never have considered in the past out of fear of being so alone. It just wasn't something the old Sophie could ever possibly do.

But after that trip to Japan with Bobby, I had changed. The idea of challenging myself now excited me, because I knew that when I faced my fears head on, the pride I felt for overcoming them was absolutely worth it.

And so, I agreed to have a conversation with the producers.

It didn't eventuate in 2020 and that's fine, because that was clearly a shitshow of a year both for me personally and for the world, and I honestly didn't give it much thought. I was somewhat relieved, in a sense. But at the beginning of 2021, I got a call saying they wanted to chat to me again about the show.

Oh, shit.

I knew this time I had no excuses.

Yes, I was again shit scared to do it, but by this stage I was far more comfortable and confident within myself that I gave it deep consideration. I was about to be one of 24 people, out of the thousands who apply to go on this show every year, to step into the world of *Survivor*. So instead of focusing on the fears, the huntsman spiders that were going to crawl over me, the intense hunger, the cold, the physical challenges and the distance from my children, I was looking at it thinking, 'What an incredible opportunity to discover even more about Sophie.'

Winning was never even a consideration, because accepting the spot was already an achievement. Whether I lasted two days, two weeks or two months out there, the fact that I was even ready to dive in and give it a go showed me just exactly how far I'd come.

Fuck yeah.

Chapter 26

I wasn't going into the *Survivor* camp completely alone, though. Each season has a different theme, and the theme of my series was 'Blood vs. Water'. Contestants go into the game with a loved one and compete as a pair, but there is only one sole survivor, meaning at some stage, contestants will possibly have to compete against their loved ones.

Originally, I was going to be cast with Jaryd, and we would be going on as an ex-husband-and-wife duo. My initial thoughts were that there's no one else in the world I would have wanted to do this with – I think he'd be brilliant at the game. He's competitive, rational, unemotional and loyal as hell. I was also really excited to give him an opportunity to show his talents and to use so many of his incredible skills that he doesn't really get to use in everyday life.

So, when it didn't eventuate (there was a casting clash with another contestant with too many similarities) it broke my heart. I wanted the opportunity for him more than anything and it was devastating for him after such a rough few years. He was really excited about something for the first time in a long time and it killed me when they said, 'We want you, Soph, but we want another family member or it's just not going to work.'

The producers asked me if I had someone else who would consider doing it and my three sisters sprang to mind. There was no way either of the twins would do it – one of them has four kids, she runs a tight ship in her household, her husband works shift work, so that just wouldn't have been possible. Her twin is the most gorgeous stay-at-home mum, with her kids clinging onto her like monkeys all the time, so again, there was just no way I thought she would do it. But my oldest sister – the one of my siblings I probably don't have the closest relationship with – is a massive *Survivor* fan, even more so than me. I called her up instantly, knowing that she'd appreciate that I'd thought of her in that moment.

She burst into tears.

'This has been a dream of mine, Soph,' she said through her sniffles. 'I'd love to do it with you.' It was amazing because it was the green light I knew I needed in order to say yes to this opportunity.

To be able to do something like that with my sister was pretty damn cool. But, if I'm to be honest, there have also been many times through my career and my life that I haven't felt like she's been the most supportive sister to me – so I did have to face some unfavourable questions from some people around me and battle some inner demons in the lead up. We've faced a lot of troubles, especially when I was a teenager growing up and she wanted to so firmly play her traditional 'big sister' role. Don't get me wrong, having been sisters now for 31 years, there is so much love and admiration. She and I were like the bookends of the family, because the twins in the middle always had each other, and I've always felt like she worked overtime trying to make us have the same bond. There's an age gap between us of six or seven years, and we have such different personalities, so at times I have struggled with that, but I instantly saw this as an incredible opportunity for us to go on the show and mend a few broken bridges from over the years – to come out of it, regardless of the result, as united sisters who shared an epic life experience together. To do that while we were both living out our childhood *Survivor* dreams . . . enough said.

~

As if going on a reality TV competition in the midst of a global pandemic wasn't enough, 2021 also turned out to be the year I fulfilled my dream of becoming a solo homeowner.

Jaryd and I purchased our first home before having Bobby, and since then I have made multiple private and business investments, but this one was me buying for my babies. I'd bought us our first family home. Never in a million years had I ever imagined myself buying a five-bedroom family home with a pool by myself at 30 years old, but it's something I've worked hard towards over the past few years, and something I've wanted to achieve for my kids' future. But oh my God, there was so much going on all at once. Within the space of three months, I was announcing my book deal and working on strict deadlines, I was buying my first home *and* beginning to renovate, plus I was preparing an insane amount of contractual work obligations and everyday social media content ready to go before disappearing to go on *Survivor*. I literally had to make two months' worth of Insta stories and posts to be posted every single day, because I didn't know how long I'd actually be in the competition for. That's 60 days of content, meticulously planned out and scheduled so that nobody online would guess that I was anywhere *but* home (it's standard practice to sign some pretty heavy paperwork agreeing to not reveal your part of the show until launch).

Oh, and I was also doing all my usual day-to-day stuff – being a mum, maintaining my relationship, putting food on the table, surviving! So while people would see me on Instagram in that time talking about PJs and going to the park with my kids, it was actually the most stressful, busiest time of my life. With my sleepwear and loungewear brand CACHIA I always wear and share new releases live on Insta, but with some new items launching in November – and me not sure if I'd still be in the outback – we had to order pairs to be specially made and delivered in August so I could pre-film for launch day from my bedroom before I left.

I also threw into the mix organising finances for a house purchase and planning a reno that would be happening when I wasn't in the state (or even contactable by phone . . .) because my renovation started about a week before I left for filming. So that was a real exercise in trust – handing over the reins to my PA to pay the invoices and manage budgets for my build. Putting my trust in the designer and building company to run it all while I was gone. Giving authority to my manager to make any and all life decisions on my behalf. And I know that really is a first world problem – how privileged I am to be able to do that – but anyone who's done a renovation would understand how nerve-wracking the experience is when you're bloody home, let alone out of contact!

It was also just before heading off that Jaryd and I started official divorce proceedings – a move that brought up a lot of sadness for me. Even though we are in such an amazing place, I still became overwhelmed with emotion as I sat on the phone with my lawyer, discussing the ins and outs of signing divorce papers. It didn't help that the *Survivor* producers had asked me at the same time for some photos from our wedding and of us together with the kids when they were younger for my character piece. Going through old pictures was like pouring straight alcohol onto a wound, as I looked back at how happy I was in those moments. It was sad because I don't recognise that person anymore – that Sophie is gone now and I was mourning her, the old me. I was mourning Jaryd, looking so happy and relaxed, and my babies when they were little; grieving for such a carefree time in our lives that was over.

But as I was sorting through those images of happy family holidays and Christmases together, I would catch myself, and think, 'But Sophie, you actually still have all of that.' We'd made a pact that we would always sleep over on Christmas night together, we'd always sleep over the night before the kids' birthdays, we'd spend Easter together . . . Nothing has really changed in our life other than we are not in a sexual relationship anymore.

Yet still, I was feeling a strange sense of regret.

What if I still love him?

What if I threw my family away?

Did I give this the best shot I could've given it?

Is it normal to feel this way?

I know we are a family, regardless of any piece of paper or any social norms, but divorce is still such a difficult thing to do, and my heart was heavy. Regardless of how amicable and respectful the situation is, divorce is still a brutal experience, and so clinical – 'You sign here, now you sign this . . .' And just like that, your marriage is over.

~

The past year alone has been an incredibly unique time, and the Sophie from two years ago – the girl who was confused as to whether she liked boys or girls, didn't know whether she wanted to stay in a marriage, didn't know where she was at or what her future looked like – she couldn't have done everything I've done in the past twelve months. Even the girl who started writing this book has evolved over the process, developing into a more balanced, mature woman. I still don't know exactly what my future looks like, but everything I did, particularly in the three months before leaving for filming, shows my growth as a person. It demonstrates not only how I've been able to work hard and set myself up financially over the past few years, but also how independent I have become. I was about to head into two weeks' quarantine, away from my children, away from my partner, about to hand my phone over, to be disconnected from the world for the first time in forever. It was petrifying, but equally so enticing – because I know what that Japan trip with Bobby did for me. I know how it changed my entire outlook on life. And that was just a holiday – this was going to be such a different experience. I didn't know if I'd be gone for three days or seven weeks, but that unknown element excited me.

A few years ago, my ego probably would have stopped me from doing something like going on *Survivor*. I would have been too embarrassed – what if I failed at it? Or what if I suck? What if people don't like me and I get voted out immediately? – whereas now, I knew I was going to be able to take the piss out of myself if I got voted off first. I knew I'd be able to sit back and laugh and go, 'Oh my God, we did three months of preparation for nothing!' I had arrived at a place where I was so confident and comfortable in myself that if it didn't work out, it wouldn't matter, because just by accepting a place on the show, I was already further ahead than I had been two years earlier. I was already so proud of myself for committing to something like that, for signing a contract to hand over my life and not know what was going to happen. My body – in its most raw state, to be aired on national TV, with no control over the outcome.

Throughout a lot of the pre-production interviews there had been a lot of talk about the prize money, but I can hand on heart say my decision to go on the show had nothing to do with the money. Whilst half a million dollars would obviously be amazing – who would say no to that? – I had no desire to be play this game merely to chase money. Money for me can be made in so many other ways. I had already won simply by taking that plunge to take part in the show, and to sign up with my big sister was only going to strengthen our large family unit.

Deciding to go on the show wasn't anything to do with being on television, either, because I didn't need that notoriety – in fact, I'd been asked to go on multiple other shows previously and had little to no interest. I was instead excited about the challenge it presented and thought it could be another way to prove to myself just what I was capable of.

My self-worth, drive and commitment to learning more about myself could never and will never be able to be measured in dollars or in fame. There is nothing I do now in life that is to impress anyone else. Anything I do, I do it to impress myself. Nothing I do is to look showy for others, nor is it to boast. It's to make myself proud – myself only. And by doing that, I make my kids proud as well.

Deciding to go on *Survivor* was a huge step in how far I've come, maturity-wise, independence-wise, my ability to trust in myself, and my ability in life. It is testament to the evolution of Sophie as a woman. The Sophie who no longer fears failure, who instead fears regret for not going after what she wants in life – and whilst I don't know what's around the corner, I still can't wait to see it.

~

When the day finally came for me to fly to Queensland to quarantine for two weeks before heading to the *Survivor* camp, I said a tearful goodbye to the kids, hugging them tighter than I think I ever have before. It was heart-breaking to leave them behind for any amount of time, but I now knew that, yes – I really could do this and the support system I had in place for them meant they'd be more than fine. I could go out there, on my own, and I would be so proud of myself – and *they* would be proud of me, too.

I waited until the last second to say goodbye, hoping it would make it somewhat easier with less time to fuss. I kissed my partner goodbye, hugged Jaryd, got down on my knees to give my babies one last squeeze before I went off for God only knew how long. As I stood up, wiping the tears from my face, I caught a glimpse of myself in the hallway mirror, and I saw . . .

Her.

There she was. The woman I'd become, staring back at me, eyes brimming with the lessons of the past few years now etched onto my soul forever. In that gaze, I could see not only how far I'd come, but how far I would go again.

I stood for just a moment, breathing *her* in. Then without another glance, I picked up my suitcase and headed out the front door.

Epilogue

The sheer number of lessons I've learnt over the past few years kind of shocks me. How exciting if this is what life constantly teaches you! I have gone through so many changes in what is a relatively short amount of time, and I've grown so much – as a mum, as a partner, as a woman, as a human. The discovery that I am attracted to women only scratches the surface of my transformation since the breakdown of my marriage; it's just one piece of the puzzle I've gradually been putting together, as is the hurt I experienced – my first painful heartbreak. It would be remiss of me to blame *her* alone for that hurt. Whilst a significant life experience – one I couldn't fathom at the time was making me stronger – it was an unfortunate breaking point after the many years I'd spent awfully confused within my identity.

Hindsight is a wonderful thing. It would've been great to know then how to recognise red flags early on, but I had to go through those experiences to learn how to identify when a situation or a relationship isn't a good fit for me. In not only relationships and friendships, but also business, you cannot ignore those flags when they pop up. You can't ignore those gut feelings telling you that something or someone is truly for you – or that they're not.

There were flags from the very start in some of my relationships. There were red flags in a business partnership that I had that completely fell apart – from the first meeting I had with them, I knew something wasn't right, but I didn't listen to my intuition. There were so many bloody red flags in my early circles of acquaintances that I ignored outright – but if I had accepted earlier on that these were just not my people, I might've saved myself a lot of heartache. But I also wouldn't have gained the knowledge that I now have.

After everything I experienced in the past couple of years, I feel that I can now go confidently into my thirties, forties and beyond trusting my intuition as my most supportive tool. Knowing the truth by how it feels. I no longer afford people energy if they aren't deserving – instead am guided by my gut, steering me away from anything that threatens to shatter my peace.

It can be hard to drown out the noise of society telling us what we 'should' do and how we 'should' be living long enough to listen to and really hear that inner knowing. I've always been open to life, open to experience – but looking back at who I was a decade ago, I can see just how truly unaware of life I was. I can say with conviction how proud I am of the person I am forever growing into. This wasn't just about realising I am sexually and emotionally attracted to women. It was about all the changes I went through, in almost every area of my life. Life threw me some of the hardest experiences I've ever encountered, just so I could prove to myself that I could survive them.

Part of my healing and evolution through my life has taught me how worthless it is to hold onto any angst. Holding ill feelings towards anyone only leaves you with heavy emotional baggage, dragging you down, the heaviness becoming painful as you carry it everywhere. While my growth has led to me losing people along the way, I live with no bad intentions towards anyone. I recognise now that I held on to some people for far too long – that little five-year-old Sophie who desperately wanted to be seen.

Even though we hadn't spoken in ten months, I messaged that one ex ahead of the Tokyo Olympics to wish her the best of luck. Some people might wonder why I'd do that, but it wasn't in my nature *not* to reach out. I knew it would be difficult watching her on TV playing in the Olympics – something we'd discussed on many occasions. But there was a much bigger picture here than the fallout from our split. I've always been able to front up in moments of significance for people, and this life event of hers was far greater than what had transpired between us.

'I couldn't let this moment in your life go by with without wishing you the best of luck,' I wrote. 'I've seen how hard you've worked to be here, and I wish nothing but the best for you and the girls. I really hope it works out for you all.' Simple and friendly.

She replied straight away.

'Thank you, Soph, I really appreciate that. You seem happy – I'm glad. Stay well.'

I can only thank her for that and for the beautiful times we spent together. Nothing can ever take away those moments, and because of her, I am now a better, more devoted and supportive partner to my fiancée, and a much healthier person than I was.

The takeaway of my story isn't, 'Leave your husband and become a lesbian.' It's to trust your gut. To chase down your dream. To scratch that itch – whatever that means for you, however it looks, you've *got* to do it. Trusting your intuition – allowing yourself to make choices based purely on your gut feeling and understanding of a situation, whether they make sense to you or not – that is the ultimate way to pay respect to yourself. Back yourself, always, because in life, not everyone will.

Nearly every day, I have people sliding into my DMs asking me for advice about how they, too, can leave a relationship and follow their truth. And it's not just women that ask; it's men, too, and people of all ages, anywhere from 18 to 65. 'Be honest in your communication,' I tell them, 'Be accepting of your feelings – whether you *want* to feel them or not – and know that you are entitled to feel the way you feel.

'The fact you're writing this to me tells me you already have your answer,' I always say. 'You already know *exactly* what you want to do.'

Acceptance is hard. And, honestly, it can be really sad, too. But ultimately, resisting life's changes will only stand in the way of finding your true happiness.

In her book *Untamed* (which clearly had a huge impact on me), author Glennon Doyle recalls being out one day and seeing a woman she's attracted to. 'Maybe in another life,' she writes that she thought to herself that day, 'as if I had more than one.' A quote I now have proudly tattooed on my back.

~

This isn't, 'And Sophie lived happily ever after,' by the way.

My life isn't wrapped up in a pretty bow. I haven't found my forever – because how can one know what the fuck forever looks like?

From such a young age, I had a clear-set future laid out in front of me. One that didn't go the way I'd once always envisaged. I'm learning now not to plan anything; to flow through life, and to let life flow through me. That way, when change comes – and it will *always* come – I am able to fly freely with it. You can do it, too.

I have found my *now*. Whatever happens tomorrow, whatever happens next year ... I know I will be okay, I know I will survive. At 31, I desperately yearn for another baby. Is that what the universe has in store for me? Will my body allow me? Am I in a position to commit to another person the life of a child? We don't know the answers to those questions. To accept no certainty in life is to hold no expectations for yourself and the life you live. You don't have to commit to anything forever. If you're not happy in a situation, you *always* have the right to change your mind. You *always* have the right to want something else. Be okay if you've found your now. Enjoy that now while it's here.

Have I found myself? No. That would be complete evolution and I'm not going to say that I'm there yet. Having 'found myself' would mean I'm done, that I'm finished growing. And I can assure you, I'm nowhere near done yet.

I want you to know though, that the most empowered moments from my life have been the ones where I've empowered myself, and I urge you to stop looking elsewhere for what you already know, deep down, is inside of you. Never lose yourself trying *not* to lose someone else. Your most empowered moments in life are going to be the ones where you empower yourself.

Find your now, be content in the now and don't worry about tomorrow.

An uncertain future doesn't have to be scary.

It can be really fucking exciting.

Sophie

About the Author

Mother of two and businesswoman Sophie Cachia is the co-founder of Australian sleepwear company CACHIA and a prominent online digital marketing expert. In her early twenties, she became known for her blog, *The Young Mummy*, and has attracted hundreds of thousands of followers on social media who have embraced her evolution as a woman over the past decade. From young mum to trailblazing entrepreneur, Sophie now leads the way for many looking to create their own path in life.